Daily
Skill-Builders

Reading

Grades 3–4

Writer
Kathleen Cribby

Editorial Director
Susan A. Blair

Project Manager
Erica L. Varney

Cover Designer
Roman Laszok

Interior Designer
Mark Sayer

Production Editor
Maggie Jones

WALCH PUBLISHING

1   2   3   4   5   6   7   8   9   10

ISBN 0-8251-4793-X

Copyright © 2004

Walch Publishing

P. O. Box 658 • Portland, Maine 04104-0658

walch.com

Printed in the United States of America

Table of Contents

Daily Skill-Builders

Reading

Grades 3–4

To the Teacher

Introduction to *Daily Skill-Builders*

The *Daily Skill-Builders* series began as an expansion of our popular *Daily Warm-Ups* series for grades 5–adult. Word spread, and eventually elementary teachers were asking for something similar. Just as *Daily Warm-Ups* do, *Daily Skill-Builders* turn extra classroom minutes into valuable learning time. Not only do these activities reinforce necessary skills for elementary students, they also make skill-drilling an engaging and informative process. Each book in this series contains 180 reproducible activities—one for each day of the school year!

How to Use *Daily Skill-Builders*

Daily Skill-Builders are easy to use—simply photocopy the day's activity and distribute it. Each page is designed to take approximately ten to fifteen minutes. Many teachers choose to use them in the morning when students are arriving at school or in the afternoon before students leave for the day. They are also a great way to switch gears from one subject to another. No matter how you choose to use them, extra classroom minutes will never go unused again.

Building Skills for All Students

The *Daily Skill-Builders* activities give you great flexibility. The activities can be used effectively in a variety of ways to help all your students develop important skills, regardless of their level.

Depending on the needs of your students and your curriculum goals, you may want the entire class to do the same skill-builder, or you may select specific activities for different students. There are several activities for each topic covered in *Daily Skill-Builders*, so you can decide which and how many activities to use to help students to master a particular skill.

If a student does not complete an activity in the allotted time, he or she may complete it as homework, or you may allow more time the next day to finish. If a student completes a skill-builder early, you may want to assign another. *Daily Skill-Builders* give you options that work for you.

Students in one grade level vary in their abilities, so each *Daily Skill-Builders* covers two grades. In a fourth-grade class, for example, some students may need the books for grades 3–4. Other students may need the greater challenge presented in the 4–5 books. Since all the books look virtually the same and many of the activities are similar, the students need not know that they are working at different levels.

No matter how you choose to use them, *Daily Skill-Builders* will enhance your teaching. They are easy for you to use, and your students will approach them positively as they practice needed skills.

Drawing Directions

Follow the **directions** to make a picture in the box below.

Title _____

┌───┐
│   │
│   │
│   │
│   │
│   │
│   │
│   │
│   │
│   │
│   │
│   │
└───┘

1. Draw a circle in the upper right corner.

2. Draw lines off the circle to make a sun.

3. Draw grass along the bottom of box.

4. Draw two trees.

5. Draw five birds in the sky.

6. Draw a picture of yourself standing under one of the trees.

7. Now write a title for your picture on the line above the box.

Pop Quiz!

Follow these **directions.** Answer the questions below. Read all of the items below before you begin. You do not have to answer questions in complete sentences.

1. What is your name? _____

2. When is your birthday? _____

3. What is your favorite color? _____

4. Do you have any brothers or sisters? _____

5. If you answered yes, what are their names? _____

6. Do you have any pets? _____

7. What is the name of the town that you live in? _____

8. Do you play any sports? _____

9. What is your favorite sport? _____

10. Only answer questions 1, 3, 6, and 7.

Derek Goes to Work!

Jonah's older brother, Derek, is starting his first day at work. Read the following passage about Derek's day. Then **follow** the **directions.**

Monday was Derek's first day at his new job. He arrived at work right on time at 9:00 A.M. Derek was brought to his office. He had a desk, chair, telephone, and computer. Derek's secretary is named Joanie. Joanie's desk is right outside of Derek's office. Derek's boss is named Ms. Matheson. Derek had a busy morning. The phone rang nonstop. At noon, Derek and Joanie had lunch together, along with two other workers, James and Nancy. After lunch, Derek went right back to work. By the end of the day, he was happy but tired!

1. Draw a circle around the names of anyone that Derek works with.

2. Underline the time that Derek arrived at work.

3. On the lines below, list all of the items in Derek's new office.

_____

_____

_____

_____

_____

_____

Scavenger Hunt

Follow these **directions.** You will need crayons or colored pencils to complete this activity.

1. Find a paper clip. Draw a picture of it in the box.

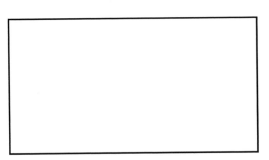

2. Write the first names of three of your classmates. _____

_____

3. Write the name of your teacher. _____

4. Color in the following objects. Color the apple red. Color the flower yellow. Color the fish orange.

Why Should I Listen?

1. Circle every third letter in the following list of letters. Then, write the letters on the lines to spell out the secret message.

O K F I E O W P L E T L P Q O R C W D X I G V N W R G E Q D S V I P P R

O F E S E C G H T T G I L M O W R N Q I S P R I M D S B Y V W Y E X P R

Z M Y T H I Q K M R T P L J O E S R M E T W F A M C N C W T

_ _ _ _ _ _ _ _ _   _ _ _ _ _ _ _ _ _ _

_ _   _ _ _ _   _ _ _ _ _ _ _ _ _ !

2. Now circle every fourth letter in the following list of letters and write the second message. Then **follow** the **directions** in the message.

R T G D W P L R T Q M A E X L W P I M A T V S S T P E A P V B I B T

D L Q X J B P E R O Z L C A W I T T A B C I C A T N D O G T I N W H I T E E

L A R B S A T O I N N X

_ _ _ _   _   _ _ _ _ _ _ _ _ _ .

State Search

Follow these **directions.** Circle the sixteen states hidden in the word search. The states are listed below. Then write the names of states that you have visited on the lines on the left side. Finally, write the names of states you would like to visit on the lines on the right side.

Alaska	Hawaii	Nevada	Rhode Island
California	Illinois	New Mexico	Texas
Colorado	Maine	New York	Massachusetts
Florida	Michigan	Ohio	Utah

```
J  M  E  L  F  K  M  I  C  H  I  G  A  N  L
F  L  O  R  I  D  A  Y  O  U  A  I  O  W  N
N  A  R  N  P  S  S  E  R  K  H  W  P  Q  M
E  Z  I  A  L  A  S  K  A  U  W  S  A  Z  I
W  B  D  N  T  I  A  L  R  E  T  C  F  I  S
M  A  I  N  E  G  C  O  L  O  R  A  D  O  I
E  H  L  E  X  D  H  K  H  T  F  L  H  A  S
X  O  L  V  A  M  U  Y  B  I  H  I  O  D  L
I  C  I  A  S  H  S  W  Y  O  O  F  K  W  P
C  X  N  D  F  C  E  N  E  W  Y  O  R  K  O
O  Z  O  A  T  B  T  P  C  B  D  R  J  E  F
Y  A  I  N  R  Y  T  S  M  A  I  N  O  D  N
E  N  S  A  A  L  S  T  K  J  H  I  B  S  T
R  H  O  D  E  I  S  L  A  N  D  A  N  Y  S
```

States I Have Visited

_____

_____

_____

_____

States I Would Like to Visit

_____

_____

_____

_____

Recipe for Disaster!

Read the story below. You will see why **following directions** is very important. Then answer the questions.

Mario decided to bake a cake for his mother's birthday. He got out a bowl, a mixer, and a chocolate cake mix. Chocolate cake with chocolate frosting was her favorite! Mario followed the directions on the box and combined the cake mix with eggs, oil, and water. Then he put the cake in the oven and baked it for 40 minutes. While the cake was baking, Mario mixed up some chocolate frosting. The buzzer went off, and Mario took the cake out of the oven. He immediately started to frost the cake. As soon as it was frosted, the frosting started sliding off the cake. He called to his dad to help him. His father looked at the warm, gooey frosting that had slid right off the cake.

"Did you let the cake cool before you frosted it, Mario?" he asked.

"No, I didn't know that I had to," replied Mario.

"Didn't you follow the directions on the box?" his father asked.

"Yes," said Mario.

His father looked on the box.

"See," he said. "It says, 'Let cake cool completely before frosting.'"

"Oops," said Mario. "I stopped reading the directions after it said how long to bake the cake. I thought that I was all done."

1. Why did the frosting slide off the cake? _____

_____

2. Why did Mario stop reading the directions? _____

_____

3. What does this teach us about reading directions? _____

_____

Favorite Foods Graph

Below is a circle graph that Mrs. Benson's third-grade class made. It shows the favorite foods of the students. Look at the circle graph, and **follow** the **directions** below.

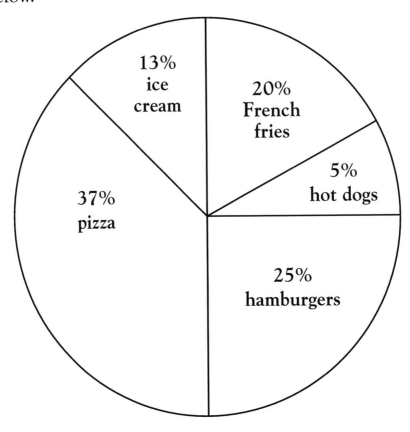

1. Color the most popular kind of food red.

2. Color the French fries section blue.

3. Color the least popular type of food green.

4. Color the 25% section yellow.

5. Color the remaining section brown.

Daily Skill-Builders Reading 3–4
walch.com © 2004 Walch Publishing

Your Own Circle Graph

Follow the **directions** below to create your own circle graph.

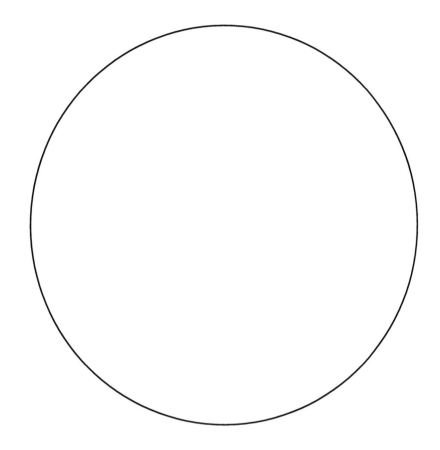

1. Draw two intersecting (crossed) lines inside your circle so that your circle is divided into four equal parts.

2. Color the upper left portion of your graph blue.

3. Divide the upper right section into two equal parts. Color one half red and one half purple.

4. Color the remaining portions of your circle graph brown.

Ordering Carly's Day

Carly wrote about an exciting day. She forgot to put her sentences in order. Help Carly by putting the sentences in the correct order, or **sequence.** Write the letters on the lines provided. Be sure to read through all of the sentences before you begin numbering.

1. _____   **a.** I left the zoo for my softball game.

2. _____   **b.** I ate dinner at my favorite restaurant.

3. _____   **c.** I ate pancakes for breakfast.

4. _____   **d.** I brushed my teeth before bed.

5. _____   **e.** I scored the winning run!

6. _____   **f.** I went to a birthday party at the zoo.

7. _____   **g.** I was very tired and ready for bed.

8. _____   **h.** I ate lunch by the monkey cages.

Birthday Cake Order

Today is Jamie's birthday, and you are making her cake. Your mother left directions, but she forgot to put them in the correct order (**sequence**). Put the directions in the correct order. Write the letter of the correct direction on the lines provided.

1. _____   **a.** Read the directions on the box of cake mix.

2. _____   **b.** Let cake cool, then frost cake.

3. _____   **c.** Pour the cake mix into the bowl.

4. _____   **d.** Bake in the oven for 35 minutes.

5. _____   **e.** Add 2 eggs, $\frac{1}{2}$ cup of water, and $\frac{1}{4}$ cup of oil.

6. _____   **f.** Preheat the oven to 350° F.

7. _____   **g.** Beat ingredients together.

8. _____   **h.** Pour batter into greased pan.

Skiing Sequence

Read the following story, and look for the order, or **sequence,** of what
Andrew did during his day. Then answer the questions below.

Last Saturday, Andrew went skiing for the first time. Since he had
never skiied before, he took lessons. First, Andrew went to the rental
department and rented a pair of skis, poles,
and boots. Then his dad signed him up to take
a lesson with a professional ski instructor.
Andrew's lesson lasted three hours. At the
end of his lesson, he met his father for lunch.
After lunch, Andrew went on the chairlift
with his dad. He skiied all the way down from
the top! By the end of the day, Andrew was
exhausted. On the way home, Andrew fell
asleep in the car. It had been a great day!

1. What was the first thing that Andrew did when he got to the mountain?

   _____

2. What did Andrew do after his lesson? _____

   _____

3. Who did Andrew ski with after lunch? _____

   _____

4. What was the last thing that Andrew did? _____

   _____

Fish Magnets

It is a rainy Saturday afternoon. You and your mom decide to make crafts. You are going to make fish magnets. Read the directions below. Put them in the correct order, or **sequence,** by writing the letter of the correct direction on the lines.

1. _____   **a.** Glue on a googly eye.

2. _____   **b.** Cut out three little blue triangles.

3. _____   **c.** Trace the fish pattern on pink construction paper.

4. _____   **d.** Glue a magnet on the back of your finished fish.

5. _____   **e.** Cut the fish out of the construction paper.

6. _____   **f.** Glue the blue triangles onto the fish in a pattern.

7. _____   **g.** Put your new magnet on the refrigerator.

Florida Sequence

Read the postcard below. Note all the things that Kasey did and the **sequence** in which she did them. Then answer the questions that follow.

Dear Grandma,
Florida is great! The first day we were here, we went to Sea World. First, we watched the trick water skiiers. Then we went to Shamu's show. It was really neat! We ate lunch at a café by the shark tanks. On our way out, Dad bought me a stuffed Shamu doll. I love Florida! See you soon!
                    Love, Kasey

Grandma Green

14 Maple Avenue

St. Paul, MN 45964

1. Where did Kasey go when she got to Florida?_____

_____

2. What was the first thing that she did at Sea World? _____

_____

3. Where did Kasey go before lunch? _____

_____

4. What was the last thing that Dad did at Sea World? _____

_____

Order on the Farm

Zachary's grandparents live on a farm. Last Saturday, Zachary went to the farm to visit his grandparents. While he was there, he helped his grandfather feed the animals. Read the story below. Then write the animals in the **sequence** that Zachary and his grandfather fed them on the lines below.

Zachary and his grandfather went out to the barn to feed the animals. Their first stop was the chicken pen where Zachary scattered seeds for the chickens to eat. Next, they stopped at the sheep pen to feed the sheep. Then, they walked across the yard to the big barn that held the horses and cows. There was a family of ducks that waddled along after them. As he walked along, Zachary dropped handfuls of feed for the ducks. When they reached the large barn, Zachary fed the horses. He filled their bins with hay. Then, his grandfather let him feed them apples out of his hand! Next, he fed the pigs. He dumped a sloppy mixture into their feed trough, and they all fought over it. The last animals to be fed were the cows. Zachary and his grandfather let the cows out of the barn and into the pasture so that they could graze on the grass. Zachary had fun feeding all of the animals!

1. _____

2. _____

3. _____

4. _____

5. _____

6. _____

Your Sequence

On the lines below, list seven things that you have done today. They can be as simple as "waking up." After you have written seven things, go back and number them in the **sequence** in which you did them.

_____ _____

_____ _____

_____ _____

_____ _____

_____ _____

_____ _____

Now, write at least five other things you will do today. Write them in the sequence in which you will do them.

_____ _____

_____ _____

_____ _____

_____ _____

_____ _____

What a Long Day!

David just got back from a long day at the beach. His mother wants him to take a shower before he goes to bed. Below is a list of everything that David does before he goes to bed. Put them in the **sequence** that makes the most sense. Write the letter of the correct answer on the lines provided.

1. _____   **a.** David takes off his bathing suit.

2. _____   **b.** David gets home from the beach.

3. _____   **c.** David turns on the shower.

4. _____   **d.** David climbs into bed.

5. _____   **e.** David dries off from the shower.

6. _____   **f.** David goes to his bedroom.

7. _____   **g.** David puts on his pajamas.

8. _____   **h.** David turns off the light.

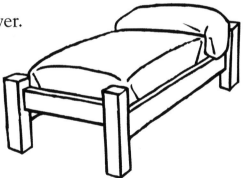

Fish Sequence

Below are eight pairs of statements. Each statement has a fish beside it. Put the statements in the correct order (**sequence**). Color the fish beside the statement that comes first.

1. Preheat the oven to 350°.

   Place the pan in the oven.

2. Get into the shower.

   Take off your socks.

3. Eat dinner.

   Brush your teeth.

4. Put on your winter coat.

   Go out to play in the snow.

5. Go to fifth grade.

   Go to kindergarten.

6. Go for a swim in the lake.

   Dry off with a beach towel.

7. Do your homework.

   Get home from school.

A Picture Is Worth 1,000 Words

A **main idea** tells what a picture or paragraph is mostly about. Look at the pictures below. Then write a sentence that tells the main idea of each picture.

1.

_____

_____

_____

2.

_____

_____

_____

3.

_____

_____

_____

4.

_____

_____

_____

Finding the Main Idea

Read the paragraph below. As you read, figure out the **main idea,** or what the paragraph is mostly about.

Abraham Lincoln was one of the greatest presidents of the United States. Lincoln was president during the Civil War. He abolished slavery. He worked to keep the States unified. Lincoln was known as "Honest Abe" because he was believed to be a very honest man. Lincoln was assassinated during his presidency. He was shot while he watched a play. Lincoln is still remembered as a great leader of our country.

Answer the following.

1. Who is the paragraph mostly about? _____

2. Why is he remembered by Americans? _____

   _____

3. Write a main idea sentence. _____

   _____

Daily Skill-Builders Reading 3–4
walch.com © 2004 Walch Publishing

Holiday Spirit

The **main idea** of a paragraph tells what the paragraph is mostly about. Read the following paragraph. Then answer the questions below.

> Mrs. Keene's fifth-grade class was trying to decide how to help families who did not have enough money to buy holiday presents for their children. The students decided to collect "almost new" toys from people in their town. They cleaned up the toys to make them look new. Then they gave them to families that wanted them.

1. Who is the story about? _____

2. What were they doing? _____

3. Why were they doing this?_____

4. Which is the best title for this story? Circle it.

   "Saving Money to Buy Toys"

   "Helping Needy Families"

   "Fifth-Graders"

5. Which sentence below would best fit in the paragraph? Circle it.

   My parents played with toys when they were young.

   Toys were collected through December 15.

   My brother's class had a car wash for a special cause.

A Maine Event

Read the following story. Look for the **main idea.** Then answer the questions below.

Mr. Bishop's fourth-grade class was studying marine wildlife. They took a trip to the coast of Maine to go whale watching. The students went on a large boat that took them far out into the Atlantic Ocean. There they watched the huge whales diving and leaping out of the water. They even saw a baby whale. The baby swam right next to its mother. The whales got so close to the boat that the students got soaked when the whales splashed. It was a spectacular day!

1. Who is the story about? _____

2. What happened in the story?_____

_____

3. Why did the class go on the trip? _____

_____

4. What would be the best title for the story? Circle it.

"A Trip to the Maine Woods"

"Watching Maine Whales"

"Ocean Fishing"

"An Island School"

Whose Idea Was That?

Every paragraph has a **main idea,** and the sentences in a paragraph should be connected to the main idea. Below are some words and phrases that could be grouped together in a paragraph. Read the words and phrases, and decide what the main idea of the paragraph might be. Then write it on the line.

1. _____

   eating cake and ice cream

   singing a song

   blowing out candles

2. _____

   lions

   tigers

   zebras

3. _____

   quartz

   garnet

   limestone

4. _____

   Abraham Lincoln

   George Washington

   George W. Bush

5. _____

   hot sand

   seawater

   collecting shells

Don't Bug Me!

As you read the story below, look for the **main idea.** Then answer the questions that follow.

Bugs are interesting creatures. They come in all shapes and sizes. Some have lots of legs, and some have no legs at all. Some crawl on the ground, and others fly through the air. Some even change form as they grow. For example, butterflies begin their lives as caterpillars. Some bugs, like termites, destroy things. Others, like ladybugs, are fun to look at. Bugs are amazing!

1. Which of the following sentences best describes the main idea of the paragraph?

   a. Bugs live in hot, damp places.

   b. Bugs are pesky creatures.

   c. There are many kinds of bugs.

   d. Bugs crawl all over everything.

2. What is one thing that you know about bugs after reading the paragraph?

   _____

   _____

Kalisha's Summer

Below is an outline of Kalisha's paper about her summer vacation. She has sorted all of her summer activities into groups. Each of these groups will become one paragraph. The only thing that Kalisha has forgotten is to write down the **main idea** of each paragraph. Read the outline, and fill in the lines with the main idea for each paragraph. The main idea should be written as a complete sentence.

   I. Introduction

  II. _____

       a. going to the ocean

       b. visiting Grandma and Grandpa

       c. trip to the amusement park

 III. _____

       a. how to swim by myself

       b. riding my bike without training wheels

       c. playing softball

  IV. _____

       a. spaghetti

       b. ice-cream cones

       c. watermelon

   V. Conclusion

Your Autobiography

When a person writes a story about his or her own life, it is called an autobiography. Imagine that you are writing part of your autobiography. Choose one special thing that has happened to you, and write about it.
Remember: Include details that answer *who*, *what*, *why*, *when*, and *where*.

_____

_____

_____

_____

_____

_____

_____

_____

_____

_____

_____

What is the **main idea?** _____

_____

_____

All About Elephants

Read the following paragraph, and look for the **main idea.** Then answer the questions below.

Elephants are fascinating creatures. They are extremely large animals. They are the largest land mammals. Only whales, which live in the ocean, are larger. Elephants live in Africa and in Asia. Elephants have almost no hair on their bodies. Their trunks are long and flexible. Elephants were once hunted for their ivory. They are now protected animals. It is believed that elephants feel grief and other emotions.

1. What is the main idea of the paragraph?_____

_____

2. What did you learn about elephants? _____

_____

3. Where do elephants live?_____

_____

4. Why would anyone want to harm elephants? _____

_____

Feathered Friends

Read the following paragraph. Look for the **details** that make the story interesting. Then answer the questions below.

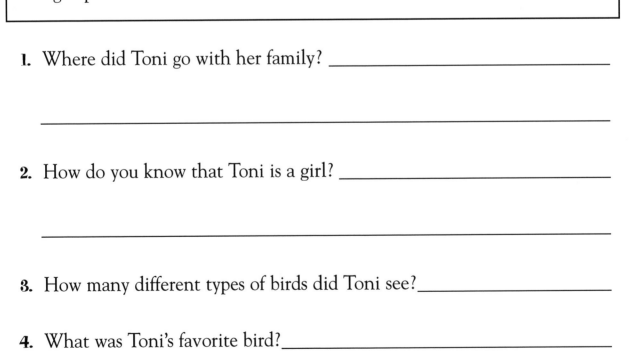

When Toni went to Florida, she saw lots of neat birds. Her family went to a bird sanctuary where Toni saw birds that she had never seen before! She saw flamingos, herons, pelicans, parrots, and peacocks. She even saw a swan! Toni watched the pelicans dive into the water looking for fish. She talked to the parrot, and it repeated everything that she said. Her favorite birds, though, were the flamingos! She loved their curved beaks and their bright pink feathers.

1. Where did Toni go with her family? _____

_____

2. How do you know that Toni is a girl? _____

_____

3. How many different types of birds did Toni see? _____

4. What was Toni's favorite bird? _____

Camping Details

Read the following paragraph. Look for **details** about Ryan's camping trip. Then answer the questions below.

Last summer, Ryan's family went camping in the White Mountains of New Hampshire. They drove to a campground and selected a good site. Then, they set up their tent. Once they had their tent up and their camping things unpacked, Ryan's father built a fire. They cooked hot dogs on sticks over the fire. After dinner, Ryan's mother took out some marshmallows, and they toasted them over the fire. Ryan ate five marshmallows! A little while later, Ryan fell asleep by the fire. It had been a busy day!

1. When did Ryan's family go camping? _____

2. Where did Ryan's family go camping? _____

_____

3. How did they get to their campsite? _____

4. When did Ryan's father build a campfire? _____

_____

5. How many marshmallows did Ryan eat? _____

Detailed Description

Details are an important part of a story. Writers use details to paint a clear picture for their readers.

Look at the pictures below. Then, write two or three sentences that give a detailed description of each picture.

1.	_____ _____ _____ _____
2.	_____ _____ _____ _____
3.	_____ _____ _____ _____

Daily Skill-Builders Reading 3–4
walch.com © 2004 Walch Publishing

Picnic in the Park

Rewrite the following paragraph using more descriptive words and **details.**

Last Sunday started out as a sunny day. We decided to go to the park. While we were there, we fed the ducks. We had saved all of our stale bread. We broke it up and threw the pieces to the mother duck and her ducklings. Then we spread out a blanket and had a picnic. Just as we were finishing our lunch, some dark clouds rolled in, and it began to thunder. We packed up just as the rain started to fall!

_____

_____

_____

_____

_____

_____

_____

_____

What would be a good title for your new paragraph?_____

_____

Dad's Chocolate Chip Cookies

Read the following paragraph. Look for **details** that make the story interesting. Then answer the questions that follow.

Every Monday afternoon when I get home from school, Dad has chocolate chip cookies waiting for me. I love walking in the front door to the scent of freshly baked cookies. The cookies are always warm and gooey, and the chocolate chips are soft and melted. I love to eat the cookies when they are still warm. They fall apart in my mouth, and I usually get chocolate all over my fingers!

1. What day of the week does the father make cookies? _____

2. What words in the paragraph describe the cookies? _____

_____

_____

3. Do the cookies smell good or bad? How do you know? _____

_____

_____

4. Now add a detail that would fit this story. _____

_____

_____

Details of Your Hand

Trace your hand in the box below.

My Hand

Now look at your actual hand. On the lines below, describe in **detail** what your hand looks like. _____

_____

_____

_____

_____

Describe Your Friend

Choose a classmate to be your partner. Now describe this person. Describe his or her eyes, hair color and length, height, and any other characteristics, using **details** that help to picture this person.

_____

_____

_____

_____

_____

_____

_____

_____

_____

_____

_____

_____

_____

_____

_____

_____

_____

Details, Details!

Below are seven sentences. Read the sentences, and circle all of the words that add **details** to the description.

1. My cat has a long, fluffy tail.

2. The sky was a vivid blue.

3. The sunflower's petals were soft and velvety to touch.

4. The doll's hair was so coarse that it felt like hay.

5. His voice is deep and sounds like a foghorn.

6. The fish had slippery but pointed scales that were the colors of the rainbow.

7. The air was heavy and moist with humidity.

8. Write a descriptive sentence of your own. Include two details and circle them.

_____

_____

Tell Me More!

Below are eight sentences. On the lines, rewrite each sentence using more **details.** This will help your readers picture your description.

1. I live in the United States.

   _____

2. John has big feet.

   _____

3. Kareem has brown eyes.

   _____

4. We went for a boat ride on the lake.

   _____

5. The mountains were big and covered with snow.

   _____

6. The dog was black and white.

   _____

7. The house was yellow.

   _____

8. It was a windy day.

   _____

What Am I?

Often, we can figure out what something is by looking at the clues that are given to us. That means we **draw conclusions** about what we read.

> **Example:** I am soft and furry. I can live inside or outside. I meow when I am hungry. What am I? (a cat)

Read each statement. Then draw a conclusion about what is being described. Write your answer on the line.

1. I am soft and have lots of cushions. I am found in a living room. People sit on me. What am I? _____

2. I have feathers and a beak. I live in a nest in a tree. I feed worms to my young. What am I? _____

3. I have scales and fins. I live in the water. People try to catch me with worms. What am I? _____

4. I am fluffy and white. People cannot touch me. Sometimes I make it rain. What am I? _____

5. I can have a hard or soft cover. I have lots of words on my pages. People enjoy me. What am I? _____

6. I have a long, skinny stem. I can smell really sweet. Sometimes I have thorns. What am I? _____

7. I am round. People hit me with sticks. I make lots of noise. I am fun to play. What am I? _____

What to Conclude?

Read the following descriptions, and guess what is being described. You can **draw conclusions** from the details that describe the objects. Then, draw a picture of the object.

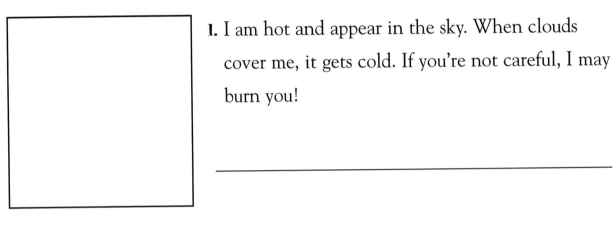

1. I am hot and appear in the sky. When clouds cover me, it gets cold. If you're not careful, I may burn you!

_____

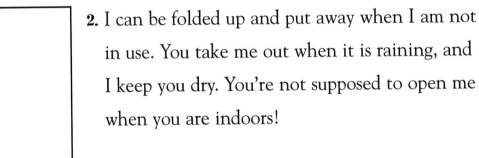

2. I can be folded up and put away when I am not in use. You take me out when it is raining, and I keep you dry. You're not supposed to open me when you are indoors!

_____

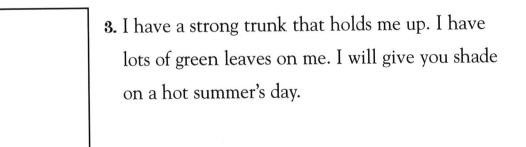

3. I have a strong trunk that holds me up. I have lots of green leaves on me. I will give you shade on a hot summer's day.

_____

Aisha's Conclusion

Read the following story. As you read, **draw conclusions** about where Aisha spent her day. Then answer the questions below.

One day, Aisha's mom told her that she was taking Aisha somewhere special. Aisha was very excited! She asked her mother where they were going, but she said that it was a surprise. Aisha put on her shorts and T-shirt and grabbed a baseball hat. Aisha and her mother drove downtown. They pulled into a huge park. Aisha's mom bought them two tickets, and they went through the gate. Aisha and her mother saw lots of fish and birds. Then, they walked toward big cages where tigers and lions were roaming around. They saw penguins, walruses, and whales. Aisha's favorite thing was the elephants. She even got to ride one!

1. Where were Aisha and her mother? _____

2. What are some clues that told you where they went?_____

_____

3. What would be a good title for this story?_____

_____

What Could I Be?

Read the sets of clues. **Draw conclusions** about what the clues are describing. Then draw a line from each set of clues to what it is describing.

1. I live in the fields.
   I have long ears.
   I am soft and fluffy.

2. I live in the trees.
   I lay eggs.
   I fly from place to place.

3. I live in the water.
   I am scaly.
   Sometimes, people eat me.

4. I grow from the ground.
   People can climb in me.
   I am green and beautiful.

5. You send me to a friend.
   I have a stamp on me.
   I must be delivered.

6. I sit on a desk.
   You can play games on me.
   I can be used to send e-mail.

- a tree
- a rabbit
- a computer
- a bird
- a letter
- a fish

How Do You Know?

Read the following paragraphs. **Draw conclusions** from the clues that are given. Then answer the questions that follow.

1. | Janie couldn't believe that her mother had bought her a horse for her birthday! She had always dreamed of having a horse, but she never imagined that she would actually own one! She couldn't wait until her party was over so that she could ride her new horse!

How does Janie feel about getting a horse? _____

Was Janie expecting to get a horse for her birthday? _____

2. | Our new puppy wouldn't get near the water. One day my father took the puppy down to the lake and got it to jump off the dock. Once it was in the water, our puppy swam all around. It splashed and chased the fish. We almost had to drag the puppy out of the water that day.

Will the puppy go swimming next time that it is near the water? _____

_____

3. | We were at the park having a picnic one day when, all of a sudden, dark clouds appeared overhead. We heard the low rumbling of thunder. The wind started to whip through the trees.

What is going to happen? _____

_____

Will the people be able to finish their picnic? _____

Why or why not? _____

_____

Name _____

Calendar Conclusions

Here is Annie's calendar for April. Annie's mother has written what Annie does on certain days. She forgot to fill in a few days. **Draw conclusions** about what Annie will do on those days. Study the calendar, and then answer the questions below.

Sunday	Monday	Tuesday	Wednesday	Thursday	Friday	Saturday
	1 dance class	2	3 flute lesson	4	5	6 ski lesson
7 Mike's birthday	8 dance class	9	10 flute lesson	11	12	13 ski lesson
14	15 dance class	16	17 flute lesson	18	19 school vacation begins	20
21	22	23	24	25 Daddy's birthday	26	27
28	29 dance class	30 dance recital				

1. Annie has something to do on April 22, but her mother forgot to write it on the calendar. What do you think Annie has to do on the 22nd?

   _____

2. On what day of the week is Mike's birthday? _____

3. If Annie's school vacation is one week long, will Annie be on vacation during her dad's birthday? _____

4. Annie is missing a flute lesson on her calendar. When is Annie's missing flute lesson?_____

5. Annie has something to do on April 6. What is it? _____

6. What date is Annie's dance recital? _____

7. What does Annie probably have to do on May 1? _____

Take a Guess

Jake is at the zoo with his cousin, Jamal. Jake is describing the animals that he sees to Jamal. Without looking at the animal, Jamal is trying to guess, or **draw conclusions,** about what it is. Read the descriptions below, and write the name of the animal that Jake is describing.

1. It's a mammal. It swims in the ocean. It makes chirping noises. It breathes through a blowhole on the top of its body. What is it?

_____

2. It has black and white stripes and looks like a horse. What is it?

_____

3. It is a type of bird. It often stands on one leg and tucks the other leg under its feathers. It is bright pink and has a curved beak. What is it?

_____

4. It swings from tree to tree. It is very playful. What is it?

_____

5. It comes from Australia. It jumps long distances. It has a pouch in which it carries its young. What is it?

_____

6. It has a really long neck and eats the leaves off trees. It is dark yellow with large brown spots. What is it?

_____

7. It is a large white bear that lives in a cold climate. It finds fish to eat and plays in the water. What is it?

_____

Why Did That Happen?

As you read the paragraph below, **draw conclusions** about what is happening to Marcus. Then answer the questions that follow.

Marcus is allergic to cats. One summer, his family rented a summer cabin. They arrived on a Friday night. Marcus and his brother were very excited to be at the cabin. They could swim every day in the lake and play baseball at the local ball field. However, by Sunday night, Marcus was all stuffed up. He could hardly breathe. His nose was running, and he was sneezing. His eyes got all puffy, and he had trouble seeing.

1. What are Marcus's symptoms? _____

_____

2. Where is Marcus? _____

_____

3. Why do you think Marcus is stuffed up? _____

_____

4. What details in the story support your conclusion? _____

_____

What Will Happen?

When we predict that something will happen, we make a logical guess. When we use clues to **predict** what will happen, we infer what will happen next. Read the following paragraph. Then answer the questions below.

Sadie's little sister, Shana, was riding her bike down the street when she decided that she didn't want the training wheels on anymore. She asked Sadie to take the wheels off. Sadie said that she didn't think that Shana was ready to ride on two wheels. Sadie said that Shana needed a little more practice. Shana begged and pleaded with Sadie to remove the training wheels. Against her better judgment, Sadie took the wheels off, and Shana began to ride down the street.

1. What do you infer will happen next? _____

_____

2. Why do you think that this will happen? _____

_____

3. What clues in the story helped you infer what will happen? _____

_____

What's Next?

Read each story. As you read, **predict** the outcome, or result, that will happen. Then answer the questions that follow.

> Timothy's family was on vacation in Florida. They rented a boat one day and took it out onto the bay. Timothy sat in the bow of the boat with his sister, Janet. Timothy leaned over the edge to drag his hand along in the water. His father told him not to lean over so far, but Timothy kept doing it.

1. What do you predict will happen?_____

_____

2. What clues in the story support your prediction? _____

_____

> Mrs. Robinson's third-grade class decided to grow vegetable plants in class. They planted the seeds in little cups of dirt. Every day, the class watered the seeds.

3. What do you predict will happen?_____

_____

4. What clues in the story support your prediction? _____

_____

Daily Skill-Builders Reading 3–4
walch.com © 2004 Walch Publishing

Predicting Plots

Titles are words or groups of words that sum up a text. Books have titles. CDs have titles. Movies have titles. Sometimes, chapters in a book have titles. Book titles give us clues about what we are reading.

Below are four book titles. Write one or two sentences to tell what you **predict** the book might be about.

1. Mrs. Jones's Class Trip

_____

_____

2. A Day to Remember

_____

_____

3. Wild and Wacky Adventures

_____

_____

4. The Attack of the Talking Cats

_____

_____

Picture Predictions

Pictures can tell a story. Below are three pictures. In the blank box, write a **prediction** of what will happen next.

Daily Skill-Builders Reading 3–4
walch.com © 2004 Walch Publishing

Super Predictions

Titles give us clues about what a text is about. Chapter titles give us clues about what the chapter will be about. Look at the chapter titles of the book <u>Super Gavin Saves the Day!</u> On the lines below, write one or two sentences telling what you **predict** each chapter might be about.

Super Gavin Saves the Day!	Chapter 1—Gavin Goes to School
	Chapter 2—Gavin Makes a Friend
	Chapter 3—Corey Is Lost!
	Chapter 4—Gavin Goes to Dramble Forest
	Chapter 5—Gavin Makes a Discovery
	Chapter 6—Gavin Saves the Day!

1. Chapter 1 _____

_____

2. Chapter 2 _____

_____

3. Chapter 3 _____

_____

4. Chapter 4 _____

_____

5. Chapter 5 _____

_____

6. Chapter 6 _____

_____

How Do You Know?

As you read each paragraph, **predict** what will happen next. Then answer the questions that follow each one.

1. Mary Ann has a dance recital on Saturday night. Her dance teacher has warned her that her new shoes are too slippery. She is worried that Mary Ann will fall during her performance. Mary Ann insists on wearing the shoes.

What do you think will happen at Mary Ann's performance? _____

_____

Why? _____

_____

2. Jamie's mother asked him to carry in the chair from the dock. It is perched on the edge, and she is afraid that it may fall into the water. Jamie forgot to bring in the chair, and now there is a storm brewing.

What do you think will happen to the chair? _____

_____

Why? _____

_____

3. Abby's mother gave her sunscreen to take to the beach with her. As soon as Abby got to the beach, she went swimming. By the time she got out of the water, she had forgotten all about her sunscreen.

What do you think will happen to Abby? _____

_____

Why? _____

Daily Skill-Builders Reading 3–4
walch.com © 2004 Walch Publishing

What's the Outcome?

An **outcome** is a result. Match the following statements with an outcome. On the line after each statement, write the letter of the correct outcome.

1. Karen drinks three glasses of milk every day. ___

2. Darius brushes his teeth twice a day. ___

3. Our dog gets walked every day. ___

4. We feed our cat every time it meows. ___

5. Maddy takes swimming lessons. ___

6. Peter practices the piano for two hours each day. ___

7. Paul reads every night. ___

8. The wind is blowing the tree branches around. ___

a. She is a good swimmer.

b. A branch broke off.

c. She has strong bones.

d. He is an excellent reader.

e. He has healthy teeth.

f. She weighs too much.

g. It is in good shape.

h. He is a great pianist.

Predicting the Future

Read the statements below. Under each statement, list three possible **outcomes** for the statement.

1. Darrin studies his math every night.

   _____

   _____

   _____

2. It rained all night long.

   _____

   _____

   _____

3. Summer vacation is coming!

   _____

   _____

   _____

4. Ginny practices basketball every day.

   _____

   _____

   _____

Cause and Effect

An **effect** is something that happens. A **cause** is the reason why something happens. Every cause has an effect.

Example: It rained all day. (cause)
The lake flooded. (effect)
Without all of the rain (**cause**), the lake would not have flooded (**effect**).

Match each cause below with an effect. On the line, write the letter of the correct effect.

Cause	Effect
1. Tran drank his milk in one gulp. ___	**a.** They wilted.
2. Lois stayed up all night. ___	**b.** He got a stomachache.
3. The baby slept all day. ___	**c.** There wasn't any light.
4. Luisa practiced the piano every day. ___	**d.** She was exhausted.
5. We didn't water the flowers. ___	**e.** Our tent fell over.
6. The battery in her flashlight died. ___	**f.** She played perfectly.
7. The wind was blowing. ___	**g.** He was wide awake all night.

What's the Cause?

An **effect** is something that happens. A **cause** is the reason why something happens. Every effect has a cause. Read the effects below. Write a cause for each effect.

1. lost keys _____

_____

2. happiness _____

_____

3. skinned knee_____

_____

4. crying baby _____

_____

5. loud music_____

_____

6. spilled juice_____

_____

7. broken glass _____

_____

8. blowing leaves _____

_____

What's the Effect?

An **effect** is something that happens. A **cause** is the reason why something happens. Every cause has an effect. Below are some causes. Write an effect for each of the causes below.

1. The tide came in. _____

   _____

2. Danny didn't study for his math test. _____

   _____

3. Kristin's softball team won the state championship. _____

   _____

4. Harry stepped on his sister's glasses. _____

   _____

5. My mom read me a story. _____

   _____

6. The sun went behind a cloud. _____

   _____

7. It snowed all night. _____

   _____

8. The dog saw a car drive into the driveway. _____

   _____

Special Effects

An **effect** is something that happens. A **cause** is the reason why something happens. A cause is something that makes something else (an effect) happen.

Read the sentences below. Underline the cause. Write the effect on the line. The first one has been done for you.

1. When <u>his mother left the room</u>, the baby cried. __the baby cried__

2. The wind blew the leaves right off the tree! _____

   _____

3. The loud music kept me awake all night. _____

   _____

4. Our cat meowed when her tail got shut in the door. _____

   _____

5. I fell off my bike and skinned my knee. _____

   _____

6. I forgot my jacket at school, so I shivered all the way home. _____

   _____

7. The pavement was so hot that I burned my feet. _____

   _____

8. The wave crashed over the boat and soaked us. _____

   _____

9. I had been walking so long that my feet hurt. _____

   _____

10. The lights went out when we lost our electricity. _____

    _____

Why Did That Happen?

As you read each paragraph, look for the **causes** of what happened. Then answer the question that follows each paragraph.

1. Larhonda was playing basketball one day with her brother. She ran up to the net to get a rebound. When she reached for the ball, it hit her hand and bent her finger. Larhonda had to stop playing because she was in so much pain.

What caused Larhonda to stop playing basketball?_____

_____

2. When Randy walked into his mother's house, his friends jumped out and surprised him. They had planned a surprise birthday party for him. Randy had no idea that they had planned it and was completely surprised!

What caused Randy to be surprised? _____

_____

3. Jackie dropped her banana peel on the floor accidentally. When her father came into the kitchen, he slipped on the peel and bumped his head on the counter.

What caused Jackie's father to hurt himself?_____

_____

4. Paula put sunscreen on when she got to the beach. She couldn't reach her back, so she decided that she would keep her back out of the sun. Later that afternoon, however, she fell asleep on her stomach.

What caused Paula to get a sunburn? _____

_____

It Makes No Sense!

Read the following sentences. Each sentence states a **cause** and an **effect.** If the effect makes sense, write *correct* on the line. If the effect doesn't fit the cause, write *incorrect* on the line. The first one has been done for you.

1. We got wet because the sun was shining all day. ____incorrect____

2. When we watered the flowers, they grew. _____

_____

3. We lost our electricity because of a thunderstorm. _____

_____

4. When I spilled my milk, my mother praised me for doing a good job.

_____

5. When I stay up late, I get overtired. _____

_____

6. I took my umbrella with me because it had been sunny all day.

_____

7. When it snowed, we had to plow our driveway. _____

_____

8. The mother picked up the baby because he was crying. _____

_____

Cause or Effect?

An **effect** is something that happens. A **cause** is the reason why something happens. An effect is something that happens as a direct result of a cause.

Below is a list of causes. Write an effect for each cause.

1. gusty wind _____

2. snowstorm _____

3. lack of sleep _____

4. tripping over something _____

5. practicing catching a baseball _____

Below is a list of effects. Write a cause for each effect.

6. seasickness _____

7. bump on the head _____

8. torn jeans _____

9. wilted flowers _____

10. crying baby _____

The Effect of Flowers

An **effect** is something that happens because of something else (a **cause**). Every cause has an effect. Sometimes a cause can have many effects. Below are four flowers. Each flower has a cause in the center. Below the flower, write two effects the cause could have.

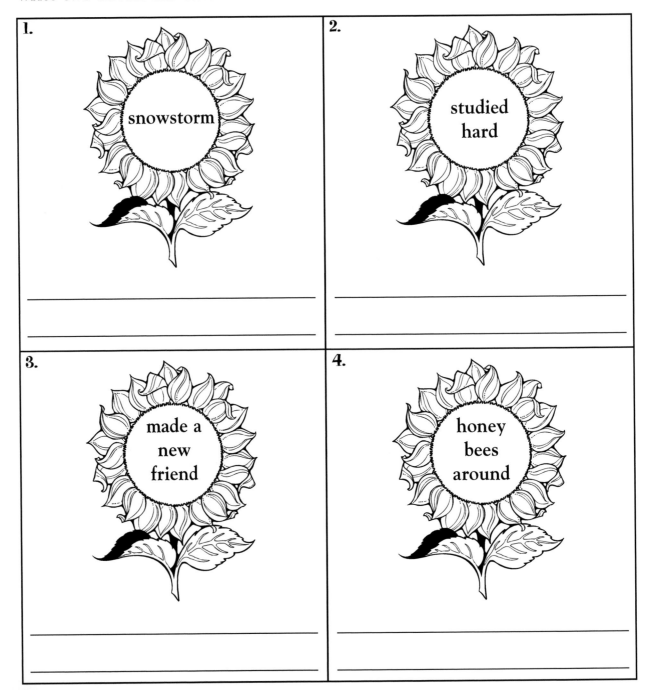

1. snowstorm

2. studied hard

3. made a new friend

4. honey bees around

Daily Skill-Builders Reading 3–4
walch.com © 2004 Walch Publishing

Fact Versus Opinion

A **fact** is something that is true. A fact can be proved to be true.

Example: Dinosaurs are extinct.
It has been proved that dinosaurs no longer exist. Therefore, the above statement is a *fact*.

An **opinion** is something that someone believes to be true. It cannot be proved. Not everyone has to agree with an opinion.

Example: Dinosaurs are fun to study.
It cannot be proved that everyone thinks that dinosaurs are fun to study. Therefore, the above statement is an *opinion*.

Read the following statements. If the statement is a fact, write *fact* on the line. If the statement is an opinion, write *opinion* on the line.

1. My name is Mina. _____

2. Mina is a pretty name. _____

3. The water in the ocean is salty. _____

4. Warm sand feels good between your toes. _____

5. George Washington was our first president. _____

6. My mother is a teacher. _____

7. School is hard. _____

8. Recess is the best part of school. _____

What's Your Opinion?

A **fact** is something that is true. An **opinion** is not necessarily true, but is believed by someone. There are seven topics in the box below. Write an opinion statement for each topic.

school	friends	math	soccer
reading	tigers	birds	

1. _____

_____

2. _____

_____

3. _____

_____

4. _____

_____

5. _____

_____

6. _____

_____

7. _____

_____

Daily Skill-Builders Reading 3–4
walch.com © 2004 Walch Publishing

Finding Facts

Below are eight statements. If the statement is a **fact,** circle the number of the box. If the statement is an **opinion,** underline the statement in the box.

1. Everybody should read <u>Harry Potter and the Sorcerer's Stone</u>.

2. Our house is painted blue.

3. Writing short stories is fun!

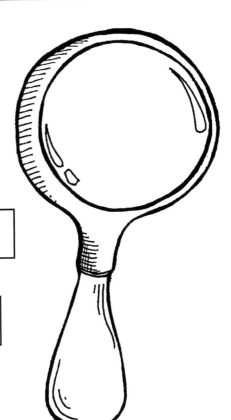

4. George Washington was the best president.

5. Wim's brother was born on July 26, 1999.

6. My grandmother lives in Florida.

7. I like making s'mores over a campfire.

8. Hawaii is a neat place to visit.

At the Dude Ranch!

Jacob's family went to a dude ranch in Wyoming. Below are a few sentences about their trip. Some of the sentences state **facts** and some give **opinions.** Write *fact* or *opinion* on the line next to each sentence.

1. Jacob's family drove to Wyoming. _____

2. They arrived on a Sunday morning. _____

3. Jacob rode a horse that afternoon. _____

4. Jacob was the best rider. _____

5. His mother was not very good, though! _____

6. After riding, Jacob went to see the cows. _____

7. The cows were not interesting. _____

8. Jacob got to milk a cow. _____

9. It was fun visiting a dude ranch! _____

Daily Skill-Builders Reading 3–4
walch.com © 2004 Walch Publishing

Give Me the Facts!

Brendan and Ethan are talking about their summer vacations. One of them is telling **facts,** and the other is only giving his **opinions.** Read their conversation carefully, and then decide which one is giving facts and which one is giving opinions.

"Hi Brendan," called Ethan. "How was your summer vacation at the Grand Canyon?"

"It was great!" replied Brendan.

"Was it fun?" Ethan asked.

"It was awesome," said Brendan. "The canyon was huge! Hiking down to the bottom of the canyon was a little scary, but I had a great time."

"Did you know that the Colorado River runs through the canyon?" asked Ethan. "Is that where you went rafting?"

"Yes," said Brendan. "The water was really cold. Rafting is so much fun! I think that it was the best vacation ever!"

1. Who is telling the facts?_____

2. Who is giving opinions?_____

3. How do you know the difference between the two? _____

_____

_____

_____

Fact or Fiction?

Sometimes we read things that claim to be **facts** but that are really **opinions.**
We have to be very careful when we decide whether or not to believe
something. Below are seven pairs of sentences. Each pair has one fact
sentence and one opinion sentence. If the sentence states a fact, write *fact*
on the line. If the sentence states an opinion, write *opinion* on the line.

1. Dogs are man's best friend. _____

   Dogs are a type of animal. _____

2. San Francisco is located in California. _____

   San Francisco is a great city to live in. _____

3. Washington, D.C., is the capital of the United States. _____

   Washington, D.C., is a thrilling city. _____

4. George Washington was the first president. _____

   George Washington was the most important president. _____

5. France is home to the Eiffel Tower. _____

   The Eiffel Tower is a beautiful piece of architecture. _____

6. You must be sixteen in order to get your driver's license. _____

   You should wait until eighteen before you get your license. _____

7. The baseball game ended with a score of 2 to 0. _____

   Baseball is fun to watch. _____

School Fact Check

Write five **facts** about your school.

1. _____

2. _____

3. _____

4. _____

5. _____

Now write five **opinions** about your school.

6. _____

7. _____

8. _____

9. _____

10. _____

11. Choose one of your opinions about your school. Why do you have this opinion? Do you think that others share this opinion?

_____

_____

_____

_____

Is That a Fact?

Below are eight **opinions.** Rewrite the statements so that they state only **facts.**

1. Bill Clinton was a good president.

   _____

2. Golden retrievers are the best dogs to have.

   _____

3. Baseball is really boring.

   _____

4. A park is a great place to have a picnic.

   _____

5. There's no better place to live than New England.

   _____

6. The best way to spend a Sunday is on a boat.

   _____

7. There are lots of fun things to do in the winter.

   _____

8. Winter is the best season.

   _____

Fruit or Vegetable?

To **summarize** means to give the main points in a few sentences. Read the paragraph below. Be ready to tell in a couple of sentences what the paragraph is about.

> Fruit is one of the major food groups. You should eat fruit every day. You should eat many different kinds of fruits, such as apples, peaches, pears, nectarines, and cherries. Did you know that tomatoes are also a type of fruit? We usually think of them as vegetables, but they are actually fruits. Some fruits grow on trees, others grow on bushes. Fruit is good-tasting and good for you!

1. Summarize the paragraph in two sentences.

   _____

   _____

   _____

   _____

   _____

   _____

2. Now, on the lines below, write a few sentences about your favorite fruit.

   _____

   _____

   _____

   _____

   _____

Summarizing Summer

Write eight things that you did last summer.

1. _____

2. _____

3. _____

4. _____

5. _____

6. _____

7. _____

8. _____

9. Now, in two or three sentences, **summarize** what you did last summer.

_____

_____

_____

_____

Daily Skill-Builders Reading 3–4
walch.com © 2004 Walch Publishing

Too Many Words

Read each paragraph below. Then **summarize** each paragraph in *one* sentence.

1. Beth loves to read. Beth reads in bed. She reads on the couch. She reads at the beach. Her mother takes her to the library every Saturday and Beth takes out two or three books. She reads every spare minute that she gets. When she grows up, she hopes to be a writer.

_____

_____

2. Leo wants to be a professional snowboarder someday. He got his first snowboard when he was seven. It was blue and gray. Leo put stickers all over it. He snowboards every weekend during the winter. He also snowboards during winter vacations. Leo loves to snowboard.

_____

_____

3. Dogs are great pets. There is a perfect dog for everyone. Some dogs are small and can fit into your purse. Some small dogs are chihuahuas and dachsunds. Some dogs are great watchdogs. Some good watchdogs are dobermans and German shepherds. Others love to swim in the water. Some dogs that love the water are Labradors and golden retrievers.

_____

_____

Tennis Summary

One of the ways that we **summarize** is by taking notes about what we read. Below is a paragraph about tennis. Read the paragraph, taking notes on another sheet of paper. Then answer the questions that follow.

> Tennis is a fun sport to play. Tennis is called a "lifelong sport" because many people play it for their whole life. You need only two people to play tennis. When two people play tennis, it is called singles. When four people play tennis, it is called doubles. Each person has a racket, and the players hit a ball back and forth between them. There are big tournaments in which professional tennis players compete for prizes. Some tournaments are Wimbledon and the US Open. Some famous professional tennis players are Pete Sampras, Venus Williams, and Andre Agassi.

1. What are the two different ways that you can play tennis? _____
   _____

2. What kind of equipment do you need to play tennis? _____
   _____

3. What are the names of two tennis tournaments? _____
   _____

4. What are the names of three professional tennis players? _____
   _____

5. Summarize the game of tennis in one or two sentences.
   _____
   _____

Daily Skill-Builders Reading 3–4
walch.com © 2004 Walch Publishing

Summarizing March

Mrs. Moore is a third-grade teacher. She has created a calendar for her students so that they know what they will be working on each week. Study the calendar. Then answer the questions that follow.

MARCH

Sunday	Monday	Tuesday	Wednesday	Thursday	Friday	Saturday
	1 Begin Dinosaur Unit	2	3	4 Dinosaur Quiz	5	6
7	8	9	10 Questions Due	11	12	13
14	15 Dinosaur Worksheet	16	17	18 Dinosaur Quiz	19	20
21	22	23	24 Dinosaur Review	25 Dinosaur Review	26 Dinosaur Test	27
28	29	30				

1. What is Mrs. Moore's class studying in March? _____

2. How many quizzes will the class take? _____

3. How many days will the class review for the test? _____

4. In one sentence, summarize what Mrs. Moore's class is doing in March.

_____

_____

A New Snow White

Read the following paragraph. Then answer the questions that follow.

One day Mr. O'Brien asked his class to perform a play. He worked with them to write a new version of "Snow White and the Seven Dwarfs." They called their play "Snow White and the Too Many Dwarfs." First the class read the fairy tale "Snow White." Then they changed the story a little—without completely changing the story line. The class made up fifteen dwarfs so that all of the students would get a part. Then they wrote the lines that each dwarf would say. Every dwarf got to speak at least three lines. After they had created a script, the class practiced the play. They practiced for a whole week. Then they were ready to perform it for an audience. Once they were ready, they assembled the whole school and performed their play.

1. What are some details that are given in the paragraph?_____

_____

_____

2. Do we need all of these details? Why or why not? _____

_____

3. Summarize the paragraph in two sentences. _____

_____

_____

_____

Daily Skill-Builders Reading 3–4
walch.com © 2004 Walch Publishing

Where to Visit?

1. Think of a country that you would like to visit. With the help of an encyclopedia or your teacher, write five places in the country that you would like to visit. Be sure to write in complete sentences.

_____

_____

_____

_____

2. Now, summarize your paragraph in two sentences. **Remember:** Include the most important information in your summary.

_____

_____

_____

_____

3. Describe some famous places of interest in your "favorite" country.

_____

_____

_____

_____

No Homework!

Read the paragraph, and then answer the questions that follow.

When Mr. Verillo came to Lauren's desk to collect her homework, she looked up at him with sad eyes.

"May I have your work, please?" asked Mr. Verillo.

"Well, Mr. Verillo," replied Lauren. "You see, last night my mom went into labor with my baby sister. She had to be rushed to the hospital, and my grandmother came over to my house to take care of me. My grandmother wanted to go back to her own house to wait for the news, so we left my house. I meant to grab my backpack and bring it with me, but I forgot to. By the time I got home, it was too late to do my homework."

1. Summarize what Lauren is trying to say to Mr. Verillo. _____

_____

2. Why is Lauren going into so many details? _____

_____

3. Does Lauren have a good reason for not doing her homework? Why or why not? _____

_____

_____

_____

Daily Skill-Builders Reading 3–4
walch.com © 2004 Walch Publishing

Let's Get Together

We often group things together that have something in common. These groups are called **categories.**

Example: Trees
maple
birch
oak

Below are four categories. Write five items for each category.

1. colors

_____

_____

_____

_____

_____

2. sports

_____

_____

_____

_____

_____

3. famous people

_____

_____

_____

_____

_____

4. animals

_____

_____

_____

_____

_____

Whom Do You Know?

1. Write the names of twelve people you know on the lines below.

_____   _____   _____

_____   _____   _____

_____   _____   _____

_____   _____   _____

2. Now group these people into **categories.** Label the categories—for example, friends, family, teachers, and so forth. Some people may be listed in more than one category.

Category: _____   Category: _____

_____   _____

_____   _____

_____   _____

_____   _____

Category: _____   Category: _____

_____   _____

_____   _____

_____   _____

_____   _____

Category: _____   Category: _____

_____   _____

_____   _____

_____   _____

_____   _____

Daily Skill-Builders Reading 3–4
walch.com © 2004 Walch Publishing

Things in Common

Below are groups of words that have something in common. Write a name, or **category,** for each group on the line.

1. green, purple, white _____

2. milk, lemonade, iced tea _____

3. <u>Finding Nemo</u>, <u>E.T.</u>, <u>The Little Mermaid</u> _____

4. mosquito, grasshopper, spider _____

5. blond, brunette, red _____

6. Boston, Los Angeles, New Orleans _____

7. Disney World, Sea World, Great Adventure _____

8. sandals, boots, loafers _____

9. ice cream, cake, pie _____

10. Dallas Cowboys, Boston Bruins, L.A. Lakers _____

11. Canada, Mexico, United States _____

12. soccer, baseball, tennis _____

Up, Up, and Away!

Below are four hot air balloons. Below each balloon is a **category.** Write four words for each category on the lines in the balloon.

1.

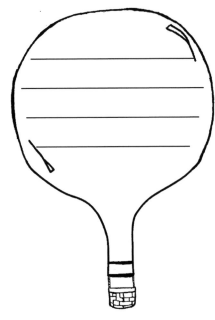

feelings

2.

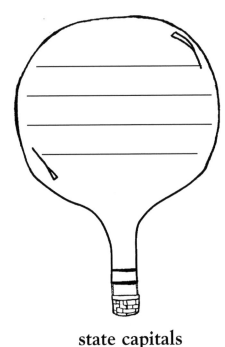

state capitals

3.

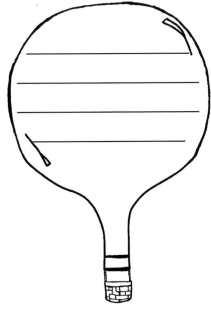

bird names

4.

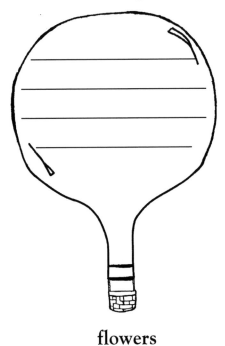

flowers

Daily Skill-Builders Reading 3–4
walch.com © 2004 Walch Publishing

We Belong Together

Below are six groups of words. Decide what the words have in common, and write a name for the **category** on the line. Then add another item to each category.

1. _____

corduroys

overalls

jeans

_____

2. _____

basketball

tennis ball

softball

_____

3. _____

fir

oak

palm

_____

4. _____

Hawaii

Texas

Maryland

_____

5. _____

golden retriever

yellow Labrador retriever

cocker spaniel

_____

6. _____

minivan

truck

convertible

_____

Making Connections

Below are six **categories.** Write each word from the box on a line under the correct category.

Mark	socks	starfish	Backstreet Boys
Pacific Ocean	Lake Michigan	Michael	milk
coffee	Mississippi River	Britney Spears	seashells
sand	jeans	soda	Paul
Atlantic Ocean	lemonade	sunscreen	Mel Gibson
corduroys	Jonathan	T-shirt	Brad Pitt

1. celebrities

_____

_____

_____

_____

2. bodies of water

_____

_____

_____

_____

3. clothing

_____

_____

_____

_____

4. beverages

_____

_____

_____

_____

5. boys' names

_____

_____

_____

_____

6. things at the beach

_____

_____

_____

_____

Daily Skill-Builders Reading 3–4
walch.com © 2004 Walch Publishing

Genres

We often **classify** books. When you go to the library or to a bookstore, the books are separated into different categories. These categories are usually determined by the **genre** of a book. A genre is the type of book. For example, mystery and romance are different genres. Below is a list of book titles. After each title, there are two different genres listed. Circle the genre that you think fits the title of the book.

1. The Haunted House on Chapin Hill
   a. horror
   b. comedy

2. Journey to South Summit
   a. adventure
   b. horror

3. The Life of Abraham Lincoln
   a. mystery
   b. biography

4. Tommy and Sue: A Love Story
   a. romance
   b. comedy

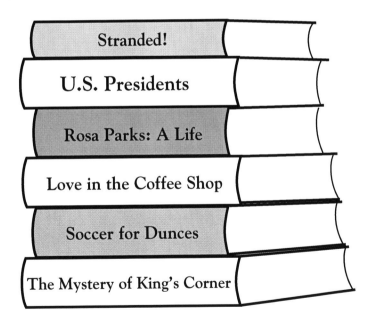

Stranded!

U.S. Presidents

Rosa Parks: A Life

Love in the Coffee Shop

Soccer for Dunces

The Mystery of King's Corner

5. What is the title of your favorite book?_____

   _____

6. To what genre does this book belong?_____

Birds of a Feather

Look at the pictures below. On the lines provided, write a **category** for each set of pictures.

Daily Skill-Builders Reading 3–4
walch.com © 2004 Walch Publishing

Same and Different

When you **compare** two things you look at ways in which they are alike.
When you **contrast** two things, you look at ways in which they are different.

Compare and contrast the two pictures below. How are they similar? How are they different? Write your answers on the lines.

Picture A

Picture B

_____

_____

_____

_____

_____

_____

_____

Livie and Jade

Read the paragraph below. **Compare** and **contrast** the two friends described. Answer the questions that follow.

Livie and Jade are best friends. They both live in the same neighborhood. They ride their bikes together every day after school. They both go to John Fuller Elementary School. Livie is in Mr. O'Brien's class, and Jade is in Ms. Mason's class. The girls play together at recess every day. Livie loves to read books, but Jade really loves math. Livie's birthday is in March. Jade's birthday is one month later.

1. What are three ways in which Livie and Jade are similar?

   _____

   _____

   _____

2. What are three ways in which Livie and Jade are different?

   _____

   _____

   _____

Sibling Differences

Miguel and his sister, Julia, are twins, but they are complete opposites. Below is a paragraph about Miguel. Read the paragraph, and then write a paragraph about Julia. Be sure to show how different Julia is from Miguel by **contrasting** the twins.

Miguel is in fifth grade. His favorite subject is math. Miguel is really tall. He has blonde hair and blue eyes. He is very quiet and shy. He is a very good student, but he really doesn't like school.

_____

_____

_____

_____

_____

_____

_____

_____

_____

Compare Yourself

1. Write a paragraph describing one of your friends. Be sure to include at least five characteristics of your friend. For example, where does your friend live? Does he or she have any brothers or sisters? Is your friend tall or short?

_____

_____

_____

_____

_____

_____

_____

2. Now, **compare** and **contrast** yourself with your friend. How are you similar? How are you different?

_____

_____

_____

_____

_____

Dogs Versus Cats

Read the two paragraphs about dogs and cats. Notice how they are similar and different. Then **compare** and **contrast** the two animals.

My cat is a wild animal! He is always climbing on the furniture and knocking things over. He races around the house every night after dinner until he wears himself out. He has really short hair that comes out in your hand when you pet him. He is mischievous and always getting into trouble. What a wild little kitty!

My dog is much more mellow. She lies around on the floor all day and is very relaxed. She has really long hair that she sheds all over the house. The only time that she really gets active is after she eats her supper. Then, she gets some energy and runs around with my cat. Other than that, my dog is a very relaxed, quiet dog.

_____

_____

_____

_____

_____

_____

Where's the Contrast?

Below are two lists of characteristics. Match up the opposites. Write the letter of the correct opposite on the line.

1. city ___

2. long hair ___

3. narrow ___

4. tall ___

5. young ___

6. small ___

7. cold ___

8. good ___

9. loud ___

10. summer ___

a. old

b. country

c. winter

d. hot

e. short hair

f. quiet

g. large

h. wide

i. short

j. bad

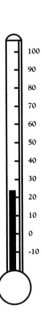

Joey's Journal

Read the entries from Joey's journal. Notice how his days are similar and different. Then **compare** and **contrast** Joey's two days on the lines provided.

Thursday, January 14

Today we went on a field trip. We took the school bus to a museum in the city. When we got there, we spent the whole morning exploring. There was an exhibit on dinosaurs. We have been studying dinosaurs for the last two weeks, so it was really neat to see all of the different dinosaurs. Then, we ate lunch right there at the museum! In the afternoon, we watched a movie about Earth during the time of dinosaurs.

Friday, January 15

Today we wrote about our trip to the museum. We talked about what we had learned from the different exhibits. At lunchtime we went to the cafeteria. I bought hot lunch. After lunch we had recess. I played kickball. It was a good day, but not as good as yesterday!

_____

_____

_____

_____

_____

What's the Connection?

When you **compare** two things, you look for the ways they are alike. Below are pairs of words. On the line, write whether the meanings of each word in the pair are **similar** or **different.**

1. | black and white | _____

2. | pretty and attractive | _____

3. | loose and tight | _____

4. | smooth and rough | _____

5. | happy and cheerful | _____

6. | hot and cold | _____

Daily Skill-Builders Reading 3–4
walch.com © 2004 Walch Publishing

At the Zoo!

Below is a **map** of the local zoo. Study the map, and then answer the questions that follow.

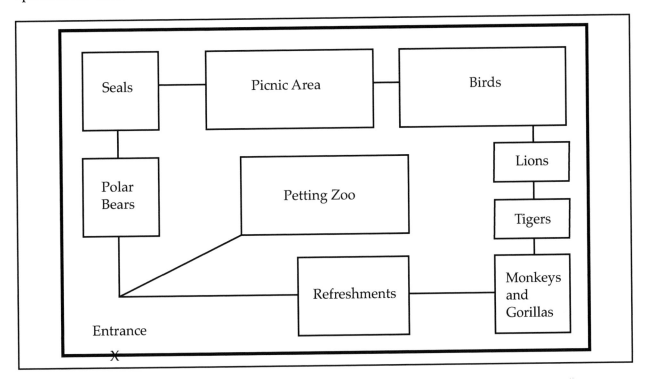

1. Which animal habitat is located closest to the entrance? _____

   _____

2. What is located between the seals and the birds? _____

   _____

3. What do you go by if you first want to go to the monkey habitat?

   _____

4. Besides lions, what other big cats are housed near the monkeys?

   _____

5. Where is the petting zoo? _____

Mapping the Classroom

Below is a **map** of the first floor of an elementary school. Study the map, and then answer the questions that follow.

Room 103	Room 104	Rest- rooms	Room 105	Room 106	Room 107

| Room 102 | | | | | Exit |

| Room 101 | Main Office | Gym | Room 109 | Room 108 |

Front
Entrance

1. Is the main office to the right or to the left of the front entrance?

   _____

2. Ms. Phu's classroom is next to the gym. Which classroom is hers?

   _____

3. Mr. Remington's room is next to the restrooms. Which room(s) could be

   his? _____

4. Which three classrooms are corner rooms? _____

   _____

5. Which room is next to the main office? _____

My Neighborhood Map

Below is a **map** of my neighborhood. Study the map, and then answer the questions that follow.

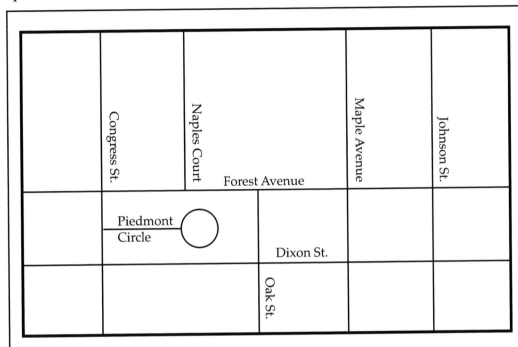

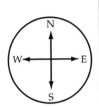

1. What street does Piedmont Circle meet? _____

2. If you are heading east on Forest Avenue and go past Maple Avenue, what street do you cross over next? _____

3. If you want to get from Dixon Street to Forest Avenue, which streets could you take? _____

4. If you live on Naples Court and want to get to Maple Avenue, what street do you have to take? _____

5. Name the two streets that run east to west. _____

_____

Charting Grades

Read Mrs. McTavish's grade book for the first quarter. Then answer the questions below the **chart.**

Student	Sept. 8	Sept. 13	Oct. 4	Oct. 17	Oct. 27	Nov. 2
Olivia	A	B+	A–	B	C–	A+
Roberto	B	B	B+	B	B–	B+
Maria	C	B	C+	C	C+	A
Kyle	A–	B	A	A–	B+	A
T.J.	B+	B–	C+	B–	B+	C
Nikki	D	B+	C–	C	B+	B
Sophie	C+	B+	B+	C	B–	C
Dustin	B	B	A–	A–	B+	A+
Emmy	A+	B+	B+	B	C+	A–
Kate	A+	B	B–	C+	C	C–
Ruben	B–	B–	A–	B+	C	B+

1. Which student got a B, B+, or B– on all of the assignments? _____

2. Who never got a grade below a B? _____

   _____

3. On what date did Emmy get her lowest grade? _____

4. Whose grades got worse over the quarter? _____

   _____

5. Which four students never got an A? _____

   _____

Daily Skill-Builders Reading 3–4
walch.com © 2004 Walch Publishing

Movie Chart

Read the movie **chart** below. Then answer the questions that follow.

Movie	Times			
Daisy's Big Day	1:00	3:15	5:30	7:15
The Mighty Frogs	1:10	3:00	5:00	7:05
The Rocking Skaters	1:00	3:00	5:00	7:00
Chip Goes to Hollywood	1:15	3:15	5:15	7:15
Coco's Big Adventure	1:20	3:10	5:20	7:30
Adventures Down Under	1:30	3:40	5:50	8:00
The Weasel and the Groundhog	2:10	4:15	6:10	8:15

1. What time is the first showing of Coco's Big Adventure? _____

    _____

2. If Hannah has to be at her grandmother's house by 4:00, what time can

    she see The Rocking Skaters? _____

3. What time is the last showing of The Weasel and the Groundhog?

    _____

4. Which movie is showing every other hour on the hour? _____

    _____

5. Which movies have a show at 5:00? _____

6. If you don't get out of school until 2:15, what is the earliest time that

    you could see Adventures Down Under? _____

7. Which movie has the latest show? _____

Charting Our Pizza

Mrs. Battey's class is selling frozen pizzas to raise money for their class trip. Mrs. Battey has kept a **chart** of the entire class. Study the chart and answer the questions that follow.

Student's Name	Pizzas Sold	Cost per Pizza	Money Collected
Mattie A.	1	$ 5	$ 5
Maria B.	5	$ 5	$ 25
Jake B.	4	$ 5	$ 20
Casey L.	5	$ 5	$ 25
Valerie M.	7	$ 5	$ 35
Connor P.	7	$ 5	$ 35
Natalie S.	8	$ 5	$ 40
Li S.	1	$ 5	$ 5
Patty T.	3	$ 5	$ 15
Zachary W.	12	$ 5	$ 60

1. How many students are in Mrs. Battey's class? _____

2. Who sold the most pizzas? _____

3. Who sold seven pizzas? _____

4. How many pizzas did Natalie sell? _____

5. Who sold $15 worth of pizza? _____

6. Who made the least amount of money selling pizza? _____

7. How much did each pizza cost? _____

8. Who sold $35 worth of pizza? _____

Flight Chart

Gertie is leaving on vacation. She is taking an airplane. When she gets to the airport she reads the monitor telling her when the planes leave and arrive. Here is a **chart** showing what is on the airport's monitor.

Flight Number	Arrivals	Departures	Status
1025	From Dallas	——————	On time
3509	——————	To Ft. Lauderdale	Delayed
2400	From St. Louis	To Chicago	On time
1017	From Boston	——————	On time

1. Which flight number is delayed? _____

2. Where is Flight 1017 coming from?_____

3. Where is Flight 3509 going? _____

4. Which flight numbers are on time?_____

5. If Gertie is flying to Ft. Lauderdale, what is her flight number?_____

6. Which flight number is coming from St. Louis? _____

Venn Diagrams

A **Venn diagram** helps us to describe and compare information.

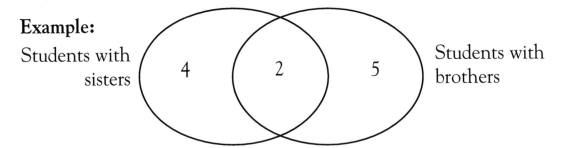

Example:
Students with sisters

Students with brothers

We can see that there are four students who have sisters and five students who have brothers. We can also see that there are two students who have both sisters and brothers.

Look at the Venn diagram below. Then answer the questions that follow.

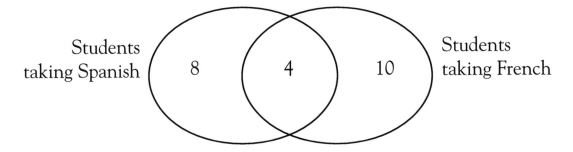

Students taking Spanish

Students taking French

1. How many students are taking only French?_____

2. How many students are taking only Spanish?_____

3. How many students are taking both Spanish and French?_____

Eye on the Diagram

Diagrams are pictures that are labeled so that each part of the picture can be easily identified. Look at the diagram of the eye below. Then answer the questions that follow.

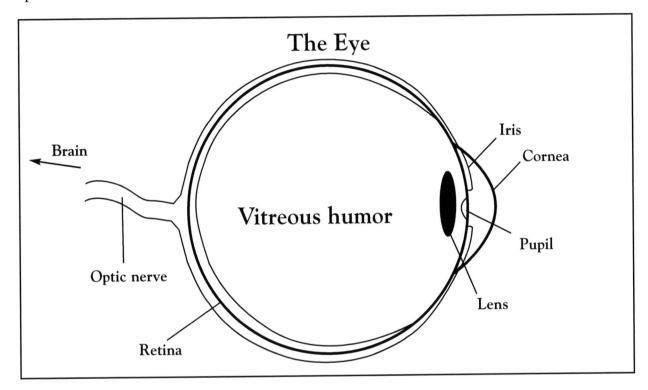

The Eye

Brain

Vitreous humor

Optic nerve

Retina

Iris

Cornea

Pupil

Lens

1. What structure leads to the brain?_____

2. What is the structure behind the pupil called? _____

3. What is the part covering the iris called? _____

4. What is this diagram a picture of? _____

Heart to Heart

Study this **diagram,** and then follow the directions below.

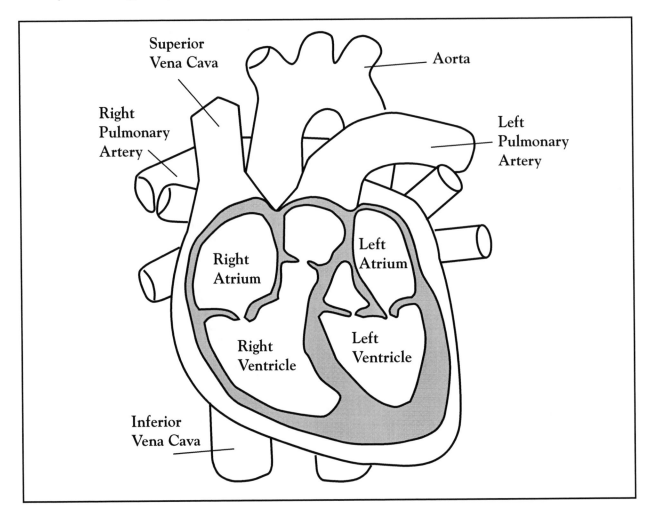

1. Color the aorta red.

2. Color the atria (plural of *atrium*) blue.

3. Color the ventricles purple.

My House

Below is a **diagram** of my house. Study the diagram, and then answer the questions that follow.

First Floor

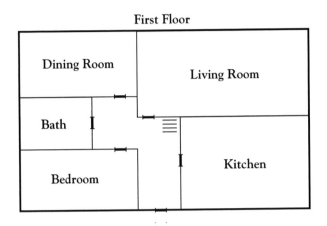

Second Floor

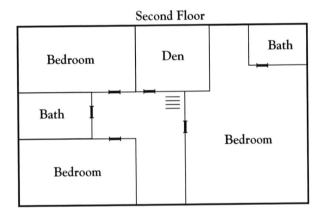

1. How many more bedrooms are on the second floor than the first? _____

2. What type of rooms are on the first floor but not on the second floor?

    _____

3. How many bathrooms does the house have?_____

4. How many bedrooms does the house have? _____

5. What floor is the den on? _____

What's the Weather?

Below is a **circle graph** of the weather in Boston, Massachusetts, during one year. A circle graph is also called a pie chart.

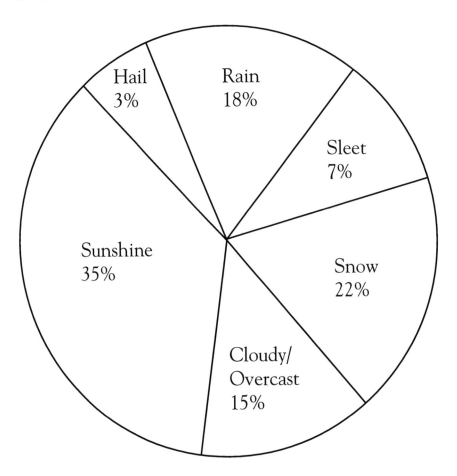

1. What is the weather like 15% of the time?_____

2. What is the least common type of weather? _____

3. How often does it snow? _____

4. What is the most common type of weather?_____

5. What is the weather like 7% of the time?_____

Graphing Progress

Below is a **graph** that shows Karen's last five test scores.

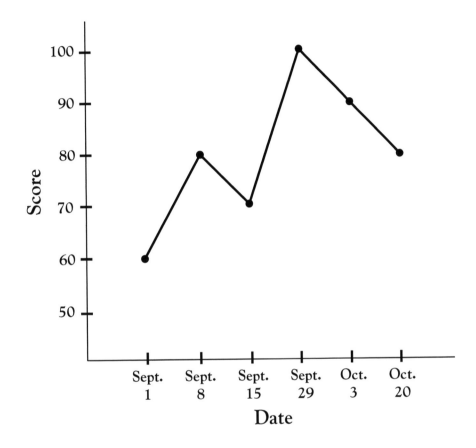

1. What was Karen's score on September 1? _____

2. When did Karen get her highest score?_____

3. When did Karen get her lowest score? _____

4. What was Karen's last score? _____

Bookworms

Ms. Wu's third-grade class has made a **graph** of their reading for the year. Study the graph and then answer the questions that follow.

How Many Books Have We Read?

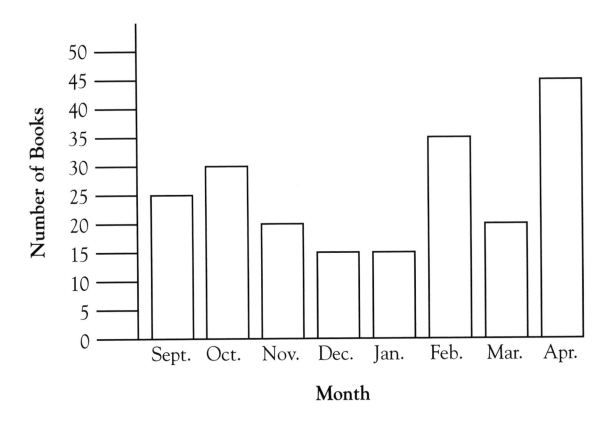

1. How many books did the class read in September?_____

2. In what month did the class read 36 books? _____

3. In what month(s) did the class read the fewest books?_____

_____

4. How many books did the class read in March? _____

Ms. Wilson's Day

Below is a **circle graph** describing the amount of time that Ms. Wilson's class spends on each subject on a daily basis.

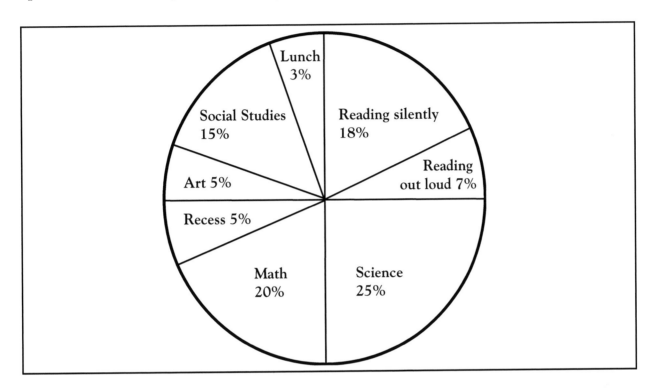

1. On what subject does the class spend the most time?_____

2. What percent of their day do they spend on this subject? _____

3. What is the total percent that the students spend reading? _____

4. What do the students spend the least amount of time doing? _____

   _____

5. Does the class spend as much time on social studies as on math? _____

6. How much time do the students spend reading silently? _____

What a Character!

Every story has characters. A **character** is a person or an animal that is in the story. Most stories have a **main character.** The main character is the most important character in the story. Read the story below. Then answer the questions that follow.

> One day, Trey had a really bad day at school. First, he arrived late because he had missed the bus. Then, he spilled paint all over himself during art class. Mrs. Cohen told him that it was just an accident, but Trey was still very upset. At lunch, Trey dropped his sandwich on the floor. When he picked up his milk, his hand slipped and his milk poured all over the floor! By the end of the day, Trey was ready to go home. What a day he had had!

1. Who is the story about? _____

2. Is he the main character? _____

3. Are there any other characters in the story? _____

4. If you answered yes, who are they? _____

   _____

5. What would be a good title for this story? _____

   _____

Zoo Characters

Every story has a **main character** or characters. These are the characters that the story is about. Other characters in the story are called **supporting characters.** Supporting characters are not as important as the main character.

Read the story below, and answer the questions that follow.

> One day, Loni's class took a field trip to the zoo. Loni was excited to go to the zoo because he hadn't been there before. His mother took the day off from work to chaperone the trip. Loni's class took the bus to the zoo. Loni sat with his friend Stuart. When they arrived at the zoo, Loni and Stuart headed straight to the gorilla cage. Loni's class had studied gorillas, so they knew all about them. After they watched the gorillas for a while, they headed over to the petting zoo. They were able to pet goats, sheep, and chickens. It was a lot of fun! Loni had a great time at the zoo!

1. Who is the story about? _____

2. Is this person the main character? _____

3. Who are the supporting characters in the story?_____

_____

Writing in Character

The **main character** of a story is the most important person in the story. The story usually centers around the main character. The other characters are called **supporting characters.**

Write a short story about anything that you choose. Your story must have at least two characters. When you have finished, answer the questions below.

_____

_____

_____

_____

_____

_____

_____

_____

_____

_____

_____

1. Who is the main character of your story? _____

2. Who is the supporting character? _____

3. What would be a good title for your story? _____

_____

Daily Skill·Builders Reading 3–4
walch.com © 2004 Walch Publishing

Character Search

Read the following paragraph. Decide who is the **main character.** Then answer the questions that follow.

> One day, Tammy the Turtle was taking a walk. She often took walks through the forest in the afternoon. She ran into her friend, Harry the Rabbit. Tammy learned that Harry was looking for his son, Georgie. Tammy was always so helpful, so she said that she would help Harry look for Georgie. They called out his name as they walked through the forest. They looked high and low, but they couldn't find Georgie. Tammy suggested that they should go back to Harry's house to see if Georgie was there. When they got there, they found Georgie sound asleep at the door. Tammy was right! She knew exactly where to find Georgie. Harry breathed a sigh of relief and thanked Tammy. Tammy was glad to help.

1. Who is the main character of the story? _____

2. How do you know that this is the main character? _____

   _____

3. Who are the supporting characters? _____

   _____

Kelly in Kindergarten

Sometimes we read about **characters** who remind us of ourselves. If the character has experiences like our own, we feel as if we can relate to him or her.

Read the story below, and then answer the questions that follow.

When Kelly was in kindergarten, she did lots of fun things. Her teacher had dress-up clothes that she played with. There was a big sand table inside the room that she and her friends would dig in. In kindergarten, Kelly learned the alphabet and how to count to twenty. She never had any homework. School was fun in kindergarten!

1. Who is the main character in the story? _____

2. Are there any similarities between you and Kelly? _____

3. If you answered yes, what are they? _____

_____

_____

4. Are there any differences between you and Kelly? _____

5. If you answered yes, what are they? _____

_____

_____

Daily Skill-Builders Reading 3–4
walch.com © 2004 Walch Publishing

Know Your Characters

Read each paragraph below. Pay attention to the **characters** in the paragraphs. Then answer the questions that follow.

> Johnny was a spoiled little boy. He yelled at his mother and refused to do what she asked. Every time he was assigned homework, Johnny left it at home—on purpose. He never sat still in class and talked back.

1. What kind of character is Johnny? _____

2. Do you think you would like Johnny? _____

3. How does the author feel about Johnny? _____

4. What words support your conclusion? _____

_____

> Caleb was really nervous about going on a roller coaster for the first time. He wanted to go, but he wasn't sure if he would get too scared. Caleb decided that he was going to be very courageous and go on the roller coaster anyway. He was still scared, but he tried to be very brave.

5. What kind of character is Caleb? _____

6. Have you ever felt like Caleb? _____

7. How does the author feel about Caleb? _____

8. What words support your conclusion? _____

_____

The Right Setting

The **setting** of a story is the time and place that it happens. Match the following statements with a possible setting. Write the letter of the correct setting on the lines.

1. When you are there, you often wear a swimsuit, sunscreen, and sunglasses. ____

    a. the park

2. You could have a picnic, watch the ducks, or just lie back and enjoy the view. ____

    b. the library

3. Here you have to be dressed warmly and have either skis or a snowboard. ____

    c. a classroom

4. This is where you sit with other students and learn things from your teacher. ____

    d. the beach

5. There are lots of books stored here. You can also use the computers here to locate information. ____

    e. a ski slope

Daily Skill-Builders Reading 3–4
walch.com © 2004 Walch Publishing

What's the Setting?

Read each paragraph, and figure out the **setting**. Then answer the questions.

One day, Milt's mom took him to an amusement park. When they got there, they bought tickets to go on the rides. Milt dragged his mom onto the roller coaster, even though she was a little nervous! They went on the roller coaster three times. Then, they rode the spinning teacups. They spun around and around. After the teacups, they had lunch. After lunch, it was back to the roller coaster for Milt and his mom!

1. What is the setting? _____

2. Who is the main character? _____

3. Who is the supporting character? _____

Gretchen's family moved to Germany when she was in high school. Germany was very different from the United States. In Germany, she lived in a little country town right outside of a major city. Many of the people in her town were farmers. Gretchen had to learn how to speak German so that she could communicate with her neighbors.

4. What is the setting? _____

5. What details do we get about the setting?_____

   _____

6. Who is the main character? _____

Describe the Setting

The **setting** is very important to a story. It lets the reader picture where the story is happening. In the box are some examples of settings. Choose three of the settings, and write a brief description of each.

Alaska in the winter	the desert
an amusement park	the kitchen in your house
a zoo	a cottage on a lake

1. Setting: _____

_____

_____

_____

_____

2. Setting: _____

_____

_____

_____

_____

3. Setting: _____

_____

_____

_____

_____

Where Was That?

In what **setting** could you find the following? Write the setting on the line.

1.

2.

3.

4.

5.

6.

Name _____

Brainstorming Plots

The main story of a book or a play is called the **plot.** Think of four books or stories that you have read recently. Write the titles of the stories on the lines below. Then write the plot of each story.

1. Title: _____

   Plot: _____

   _____

2. Title: _____

   Plot: _____

   _____

3. Title: _____

   Plot: _____

   _____

4. Title: _____

   Plot: _____

   _____

Haunted Plot

Read the following paragraph. Determine the **plot** of the story. Then answer the questions that follow.

> Every Halloween, Nate and his friends sneak to the outskirts of town to visit the haunted house. The haunted house is an old, abandoned building that no one has lived in for years. After the last owner died in the house, no one wanted to move in. Legend has it that the ghost of the owner, Mr. Singh, still lives in the house. Nate and his friends sneak into the house every year, hoping to see the ghost of Mr. Singh.

1. What is the plot? _____

_____

2. Who is the main character?_____

3. Write four sentences to continue the plot of the story.

_____

_____

_____

_____

_____

Your Own Book

When you go to the library or the bookstore and you look for a book, how do you know what the story is about? Usually, there is a summary of the story written on either the back of the book or inside the jacket cover. Imagine that you have written your own book. Now you must create a jacket cover for your book. Draw a picture on the front cover. Write a summary of your story on the back cover.

Front Cover

Back Cover

What is the **plot** of your story? _____

_____

_____

_____

_____

Daily Skill-Builders Reading 3–4
walch.com © 2004 Walch Publishing

Plotting Books

Match the book titles on the left with the appropriate **plots** on the right.
Write the number of the correct titles on the lines provided.

Title

1. <u>Cassie's Big Trip</u>

2. <u>The Mansion on Murphy Street</u>

3. <u>The Crow and the Caterpillar</u>

4. <u>Gilly Goes to Camp</u>

5. <u>Marvin's Magical Mystery</u>

Plot

a. _____ Two friends set out in search of the perfect tree in which to build their home.

b. _____ A boy searches for the truth about his special abilities.

c. _____ A girl travels to East Asia and befriends a baby elephant.

d. _____ A ghost haunts a family's new home.

e. _____ A boy has summer adventures away from home.

6. Now, make up your own book title._____

_____

7. What is the plot of your story?_____

_____

_____

Plot Sequence

A **plot** often follows a special sequence. There are five main parts to the plot sequence. The first, the **exposition,** introduces or explains what is going on. The second, called the **rising action,** is any action leading to the climax. The **climax** is the part of the story during which a key event happens. It is the point at which the story peaks. Next is the **falling action,** any action that happens after the climax. Finally, there is a **resolution,** the conclusion of the story. All loose ends are tied up in the resolution.

Imagine the plot sequence looking like this.

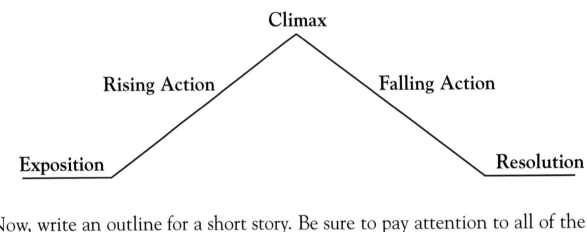

Now, write an outline for a short story. Be sure to pay attention to all of the elements of the plot sequence.

_____

_____

_____

_____

_____

_____

What is the climax of your story?

_____

Who's Talking?

Point of view tells us who is telling the story. Most things that we read are written in the **third person.** This means that the author tells about what happens to others. The author doesn't use *I.*

      Examples: Jamie ran across the street.
                   She asked if **she** could go to the movies.

Sometimes, things are written in the **first person.** This is when the speaker uses *I* or *me.*

      Examples: **I** wish we could go swimming.
                   Don't look at **me** like that!

Read the sentences below. If the sentence is written in the first person, write **first** on the line. If the sentence is written in the third person, write **third** on the line.

1. Crystal loves to play tennis. _____

2. I read every book I can get my hands on. _____

3. Dante's dog barks all the time. _____

4. He shouldn't leave his bike in the driveway. _____

5. I loved that movie! _____

6. Did Joseph leave his bathing suit at home? _____

7. I want to learn how to snowboard. _____

8. Yesterday I stubbed my toe. _____

Australian Point of View

Imagine that your teacher has given you a name of a pen pal from Australia. Write a letter to your pal telling him or her about yourself.

● Dear Pen Pal, _____
● _____
● _____
● _____
● _____
● _____
● _____
● _____
● _____
● _____
● _____
● _____
● _____
● _____
● _____
● _____
● _____
●   Your pen pal,
● _____
● _____

Now, look back at your letter. Is it written in the first person or the third

person? _____

View from the Sky

Below are a group of clouds with sentences in them. If the sentence is written from the **first-person point of view,** circle the number of the cloud. If it is in the **third person,** underline the sentence in the cloud.

1. I want to go!

2. He said no.

3. The cat meowed loudly.

4. I love pizza!

5. She doesn't like spinach.

6. He needs a haircut.

7. Wait for me!

8. Maura went to the beach.

9. I am sad today.

What's the Point of View?

Write three sentences from each **point of view.**

First-Person Point of View

1. _____

   _____

2. _____

   _____

3. _____

   _____

Third-Person Point of View

4. _____

   _____

5. _____

   _____

6. _____

   _____

Daily Skill-Builders Reading 3–4
walch.com © 2004 Walch Publishing

View from the Big Top

Read the story below. This story is written from the **third-person point of view.** Notice the author does not use *I* or *me*. The author writes about the circus as it is experienced by someone else.

One day last fall, Jessica went to the circus with her family. She had never been to the circus before. There was a big show under the tent. Jessica saw people swinging from trapezes. She saw girls riding horses around the ring while doing tricks. She saw clowns, elephants, and tigers jumping through fire hoops. Jessica had a great time at the circus.

Read each sentence below. If a sentence is written in the **first person,** write **1** on the line. If it is written in the **third person,** write **3** on the line.

1. _____ The circus is a fun place to visit.

2. _____ The tigers scare me!

3. _____ He thought the clowns were really funny.

4. _____ I wish I could swing from a trapeze!

5. _____ Jessica can't wait to go to the circus again.

Plymouth Rock

Read the following story. Think about the **point of view** of the story. Then answer the questions that follow.

> Last summer, Jordan's family went to Plymouth Rock. They drove to Plymouth, Massachusetts, on Saturday afternoon. When they got there, they parked their car down by the ocean. They walked over to look at Plymouth Rock.
>
> "Let me take your picture," Jordan's mom said.
>
> Jordan and her brother stood in front of the rock while their mother took their picture. Then they walked down to the replica of the *Mayflower*. They bought tickets and toured the ship.
>
> "Look at this, Mom," Jordan cried. "The mast on this ship is huge!"
>
> "Be careful, Jordan," said her father. "The deck is a little slippery."
>
> After they toured the ship, Jordan's family went to the gift shop to buy some souvenirs.

1. What point of view is the narrator using? _____

2. How many speakers are there? _____

3. Who is the first person to speak? _____

4. How do we know that Jordan is a girl? _____

5. Who is the last person to speak? _____

Daily Skill-Builders Reading 3–4
walch.com © 2004 Walch Publishing

Who Said That?

Read the sentences below, and find the **point of view.** The word in bold letters is a **pronoun.** A pronoun takes the place of a noun. To whom does the pronoun refer? Write your answer on the line.

1. Walter went to California last year. **He** had a great time. ___Walter___

2. My mother and I are going to the movies on Saturday. **We** are going to get popcorn and candy! _____

3. Jacinta and Jeff are great friends. **They** play basketball together.

    _____

4. Mrs. Peterson asked the students to stop talking, but **they** didn't listen to her. _____

5. I really want to learn how to read. Will you help **me?** _____

6. Luci is an excellent tennis player. Have you ever seen **her** play?

    _____

7. My mom and dad go out to dinner every Friday night. **They** have done it for years. _____

8. I can't find my sneakers. Have you seen **them?**_____

Theme Stealing

The **theme** of a story is the statement that a story is trying to make. The theme is usually a statement about life. Read the following story. Then answer the questions that follow.

> One day, Justin went shopping with his mother. Justin really wanted a pack of gum, but his mother told him no. Justin was very upset. He really wanted the gum. He thought that he should be able to have it, even though his mother had said no. Justin needed money to buy the gum, but he didn't have any. So, Justin decided that he would just put the pack of gum in his pocket. Justin took the gum, but his mother caught him. She explained to him that it was wrong to steal from the store. He returned the pack of gum and apologized to the store clerk. Justin felt really bad about taking the gum without paying for it. He decided that he would never steal again.

1. What is the theme of the story?_____

_____

2. How do you know that this is the theme?

_____

3. What would be a good title for this story?

_____

Daily Skill-Builders Reading 3–4
walch.com © 2004 Walch Publishing

Theme Versus Tone

Theme can be related to **tone**, but they are not the same thing. If a story makes you feel sad, it probably has a sad tone. If a story is about a little boy who is sad, then the theme may be about the boy's feelings of sadness. Several tones are listed below. Write a theme statement to go with each tone. The first one has been done for you.

1. **nervous**

   Theme: _Not studying for a test can harm your chances_
   of doing well.

2. **sadness**

   Theme: _____

   _____

3. **anger**

   Theme: _____

   _____

4. **excitement**

   Theme: _____

   _____

5. **scary**

   Theme: _____

   _____

Your Theme Is . . .

Some stories are about friendship. On the lines below, write a short story about friendship. First, think of a theme statement. Then write a story that supports your theme.

_____

_____

_____

_____

_____

_____

_____

_____

_____

_____

_____

Writing to the Theme

Write a **theme** for stories with the following topics.

1. friendship _____

   _____

   _____

2. family _____

   _____

   _____

3. honesty _____

   _____

   _____

4. loyalty _____

   _____

   _____

Why Read the Book?

In the boxes below are summaries of four books. Choose a topic from the box that fits the story. Then write a possible theme for each book on the line.

| family | friendship | honesty | patriotism |

1. Donny and Cindy are leaving for a trip to the midwest. They plan to visit different family members along the way. Donny and Cindy have arranged the whole trip around seeing their family. They are looking forward to spending some quality time with people they have not seen in a long time.

Topic: _____
Theme: _____

2. Lance has a big math test coming up. He has studied all week long, but is worried that he still may not pass. He is seriously thinking about cheating on his test. Find out what happens when his sister discovers his plan.

Topic: _____
Theme: _____

3. Mary's husband is in the Navy. He has just left for a three-month trip to Europe. Mary is sad to see him go, but she is very proud of his work with the Navy. She keeps a flag on her desk at work to remind her of how important her husband's job is.

Topic: _____
Theme: _____

4. Lyddie and Dawn have been best friends since kindergarten. When Johnna moves to town, Lyddie becomes her best friend. Dawn sees that Johnna does mean things behind Lyddie's back. Lyddie just thinks Dawn is jealous. Dawn decides to take action to help her old friend.

Topic: _____
Theme: _____

Showing Tone

What is tone? **Tone** is the feeling or emotion that a story has. The tone should make the reader feel a certain way, such as happy, sad, exciting, scary, and so on. A story can have lots of different tones.

Below are some different tones. Write one or two sentences that show the tone. The first one has been done for you.

1. **Worried**

   Oh no! I forgot my homework at home. I hope that Mrs. James doesn't get upset with me.

2. **Excited**

   _____

   _____

3. **Sad**

   _____

   _____

4. **Nervous**

   _____

   _____

5. **Fearful**

   _____

   _____

Watch Your Tone!

Tone is the feeling or emotion that a story has. Read the sentences below. Then write the tone on the line.

1. Wow! I can't believe that the magician was able to do that! He pulled cards out of his hat and napkins out of his sleeve. What a cool trick!

   _____

2. I am surprised at how windy it is on the water. I really don't want to ride in the boat right now. It is much too dangerous.

   _____

3. Tomorrow is my birthday! Last night I saw my mom wrapping my presents! I can't wait to open them. I wonder what I am getting.

   _____

4. I can't believe that you broke my bike! I asked you not to ride it. Now I can't ride to Jane's house!

   _____

5. Did you know that we were having a test today? I forgot to do my homework, so I didn't know anything that was on the test! What if I failed? Will my grade go down?

   _____

The Right Tone

Match each phrase below with a **tone** on the right. Write the letter of the correct tone on the line provided.

1. Wow! What a fantastic roller coaster! It was both scary and fun! _____

2. I wish that pigs really could fly! Wouldn't it be funny to see pigs flying around with the birds? _____

3. I studied hard for a week before that test, and I still failed it. Why can't I ever get a good grade? _____

4. We are going to Disney World during February vacation. It will be cool to see Mickey and Minnie Mouse in person. _____

5. My grandmother moved to Arizona last summer. She used to live next door, and now she lives so far away. I hardly ever get to see her anymore. I really miss her. _____

6. It's my birthday, and I get to have a big birthday party! We are going to have cake and ice cream and play lots of games! I can't wait! _____

a. frustrated

b. sad

c. excited

d. happy

e. silly

f. thrilled

Tone It Down!

"Read" the **tone** on the faces below. Write the tone on the first line. Then write a few sentences that express the tone.

1.

2.

_____

_____

_____

_____

_____

_____

_____

_____

3.

4.

_____

_____

_____

_____

_____

_____

_____

_____

Daily Skill-Builders Reading 3–4
walch.com © 2004 Walch Publishing

Why Do We Read?

Instructions tell us how to do something. Sometimes we read because we need to learn how to do something. Look at the list below. Circle the items that might be read for instruction.

novel	textbook	map
cookbook	poem	atlas
phonebook	magazine	owner's manual
worksheet	short story	picture book
encyclopedia	sheet music	board game rules

List three things that you often read for instruction. _____

_____

_____

Why Read That?

Read the list below. Write the **purpose** for reading each item on the line. Use the purposes in the box below to help you. There may be more than one answer.

| enjoyment | information | instruction |

1. a magazine _____

2. a novel _____

3. a street sign _____

4. a telephone book _____

5. the back of a cake-mix box _____

6. a newspaper _____

7. the label on a medicine bottle _____

8. a bus schedule _____

What Genre?

There are many different types of books, called **genres.** Books are divided into two main genres, **fiction** and **nonfiction.** Fiction stories are not based on facts. Nonfiction stories are based on actual facts or events. Read the definitions of the genres below. Then write the genre on the line next to each book title.

Fiction
> **adventure**—tells about an exciting or dangerous journey or event
> **fantasy**—set in made-up worlds with made-up characters
> **historical fiction**—set in a previous time period, using some actual people or events as part of the made-up story
> **mystery**—has clues, crime, and detectives

Nonfiction
> **autobiography**—written by a person about his or her own life
> **biography**—written about a person by someone other than that person

1. Casey's Crazy Capers _____

2. The Wonderful World of Wizardry _____

3. The Life of Betsy Ross _____

4. My Life by Betsy Ross _____

5. The Mystery of Canoby Hall _____

6. The Journey of Jezebel Jones _____

7. Gnomes and Fairies _____

8. The Case of the Missing Planet _____

Hunt for Genres

Look around your classroom. Write the titles of five books that belong to different genres. Use the list of genres below to help you.

fantasy	historical fiction	biography
mystery	autobiography	adventure

1. _____

2. _____

3. _____

4. _____

5. _____

Now write why you would read each of these books on the lines below.

1. _____

2. _____

3. _____

4. _____

5. _____

Daily Skill-Builders Reading 3–4
walch.com © 2004 Walch Publishing

Find a Better Word

Sometimes we use the same words over and over again because they are familiar. It is good to try to use lots of different words that have the same or similar meanings. Good **word choice** will help to add interest to your writing.

Read each sentence below. Replace the underlined word with another word that has similar meaning. Write the new word on the line. You may use a dictionary or thesaurus for help.

1. Milo is a good dog. _____

2. It is really hot out today. _____

3. What a nice day. _____

4. That dress is pretty. _____

5. I am tired. _____

6. That was a cool movie. _____

7. The clouds are moving slowly across the sky. _____

8. Could you please speak softly? _____

Word Scoops

Below are six filled ice-cream cones. In each cone is a word. In each scoop of ice cream, write a word that could replace the word at the bottom. Make good **word choices.**

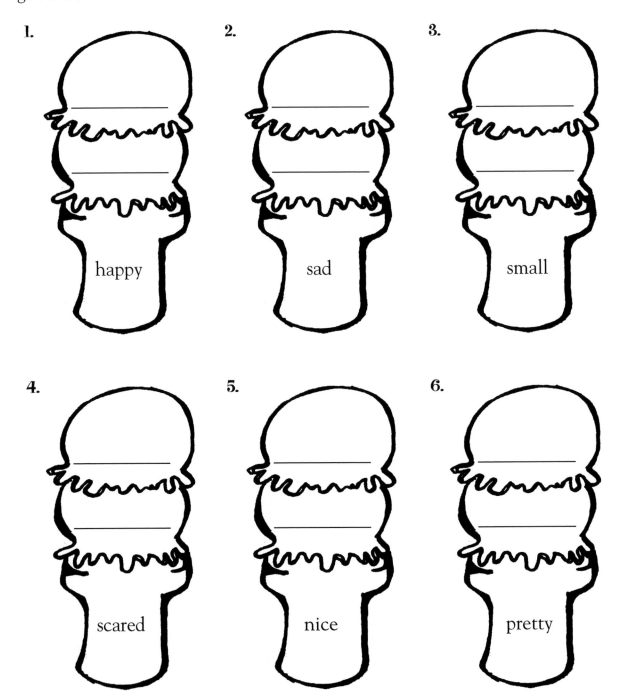

1.

happy

2.

sad

3.

small

4.

scared

5.

nice

6.

pretty

More Words

In each group of sentences below, a word is missing. Read the sentences and think of five words you could use to complete the sentence. Write the words on the lines provided.

1. Today is a(n) _____ day. It is snowing like crazy!
The wind is blowing, and everything in our yard is buried in snow.

   _____

   _____

   _____

   _____

   _____

2. That dog is so _____. The dog licks everyone it meets! It would definitely not be a good watchdog!

   _____

   _____

   _____

   _____

   _____

3. What a(n) _____ book! The main character was so smart! And I never could figure out what was going to happen next.

   _____

   _____

   _____

   _____

   _____

Does It Fit?

Read the following sentences. Circle the word that best fits into the sentence.

1. Carolyn often goes _____ with her dad. He puts the worm on the hook, and she casts the line. Sometimes she even catches something!
   a. swimming
   b. fishing
   c. shopping

2. When Mike was finished wrapping the present, he tied a neat _____ on the top.
   a. bow
   b thread
   c. rope

3. I really want to go to the _____. We'll get popcorn and soda.
   a. library
   b. gym
   c. movies

4. Don't sit in that _____! It is old, and it may break.
   a. chair
   b. bed
   c. blanket

5. Our dog _____ all the time. It has gotten so bad that our neighbors have asked us to keep the dog inside.
   a. eats
   b. sleeps
   c. barks

Word Sense

Sometimes, an author will use certain words because they appeal to the **senses—taste, touch, smell, sight,** and **sound.** This makes the story more interesting to the reader.

Read the following statements. What sense do you think the author wants to appeal to? Write the sense on the line.

1. The sun was so bright that it hurt my eyes._____

2. The dog's hair was so coarse it scratched my leg. _____

3. I love it when I walk into my mother's house and am surrounded by the aroma of warm, gooey chocolate chip cookies. _____

4. Don't yell so loudly! You're hurting my ears! _____

5. I love the first bite of warm, apple pie when it slides down my throat.

   _____

6. Now, write two of your own sentences that appeal to the senses.

   _____

   _____

   _____

   _____

That Figures!

Similes and metaphors are used by authors to make their writing more interesting.

A **simile** is a comparison of two things using the word *like* or *as*.
    Example: Her eyes were **as** blue **as** the ocean.
              His hands shook **like** leaves on a tree.

A **metaphor** is a comparison of two things without any words of comparison (*like* or *as*).
    Example: His hands were shriveled up old potatoes.

Read the following statements. Decide whether they are similes or metaphors. Write *simile* or *metaphor* on the line.

1. The sun was a deep yellow marble hanging in the sky. _____

2. She smiled like a flower bursting into bloom. _____

3. The cat's meow was like a soft melody to our ears. _____

4. My love is a deep, flowing river. _____

5. His eyes were blue like a summer sky. _____

6. She jumped off the sofa like a jack-in-the-box! _____

7. Her dress was a glowing pink tuft of cotton candy. _____

8. Her lips were as red as a fresh summer strawberry. _____

Daily Skill-Builders Reading 3–4
walch.com © 2004 Walch Publishing

A Is for Alliteration

Alliteration is a figure of speech. It is the repetition of consonant sounds at the beginning of neighboring words.

Example: Peter Piper picked a peck of pickled peppers.
Notice that the *p* sound is repeated over and over again.

Read the following sentences. If the sentence has alliteration, write the consonant that is repeated. If the sentence does not have alliteration, write **none** on the line.

1. Sarah skipped down the street. _____

2. Clara caught the biggest catfish in Corinth Pond. _____

3. Nolan went fishing with me last Saturday. _____

4. Nora needs new shoes from Neiman Marcus. _____

5. Paolo picked a bunch of purple petunias. _____

6. Now, write two of your own sentences using alliteration.

_____

_____

_____

_____

Onomato . . . What?

Another type of figurative language is called **onomatopoeia.** Onomatopoeia is the use of words that sound like the thing or action they name.

Examples: buzz and **pow!**

Read the words below. Circle the words that demonstrate onomatopoeia.

clang	kick	tick
zoom	bang	walk
please	run	click
pop	cat	hit
slap	boom	trip
wow	cut	ouch

Can you think of any other words that show onomatopoeia? Write some examples on the lines below.

_____

_____

_____

_____

_____

Daily Skill-Builders Reading 3–4
walch.com © 2004 Walch Publishing

Figure It Out

Below are seven sentences. On the line, write the **figure of speech** each sentence contains.

1. My grandmother's hair is as white as a fresh blanket of new snow.

   _____

2. Why would you wait for William when Warren is ready?

   _____

3. That fly won't stop buzzing around my head!

   _____

4. The flowers are a soft blanket of color in the field.

   _____

5. Melissa made a marvelous feast of macaroni, meatballs, and mushrooms.

   _____

6. The clock bell kept clanging the time.

   _____

7. His shirt was as green as the lawn behind our house.

   _____

Idioms

An idiom is a common expression. They are often used in conversation, on television, and in the movies. Idioms can sometimes be confusing because their meaning is not to be taken literally.

Here are some common idioms. Read each idiom. Then write the meaning on the line.

1. cat got one's tongue _____

2. get up on wrong side of bed _____

3. hit the hay _____

4. knock on wood _____

5. like a chicken with its head cut off _____

6. put on your thinking cap _____

7. raining cats and dogs _____

8. tie the knot _____

Go Figure!

Below is an example of **simile, metaphor, alliteration,** and **onomatopoeia.**
Write the type of figurative language on the line beside each sentence.

1. Mandy eats melon at Monique's house on Mondays. _____

2. His hair was as black as coal. _____

3. My sadness is a crushing boulder. _____

4. The balloon popped when it hit the ceiling. _____

Now, write your own example of each type of figurative language.

5. simile: _____

_____

6. metaphor: _____

_____

7. alliteration: _____

_____

8. onomatopoeia: _____

_____

Name _____

Baby ABCs

Keisha's mom is having a baby boy. Keisha's family has written all of the baby names that they like. Read the names below. Rewrite them in **alphabetical order** on the lines provided.

Darnell	Connor	Jordan
Johnathan	Omar	Ramon
Mark	Matthew	Garrett
Alex	Tyson	Ethan
Malcolm	Anthony	Pedro

1. _____
2. _____
3. _____
4. _____
5. _____
6. _____
7. _____
8. _____
9. _____
10. _____
11. _____
12. _____
13. _____
14. _____
15. _____

Daily Skill-Builders Reading 3–4
walch.com © 2004 Walch Publishing

Alphabetizing States

Alphabetize the states that begin with the following letters.

1. A

_____

_____

_____

_____

2. C

_____

_____

_____

3. I

_____

_____

_____

_____

_____

_____

4. M

_____

_____

_____

_____

_____

_____

_____

_____

Third-Grade Names

Mrs. Merrill has a grade book in which she writes all of her students' names. She has written the names in the book, but she forgot to alphabetize them. Place numbers next to the names so that the names are in **alphabetical order.** Alphabetize the last names, and don't worry about the first names.

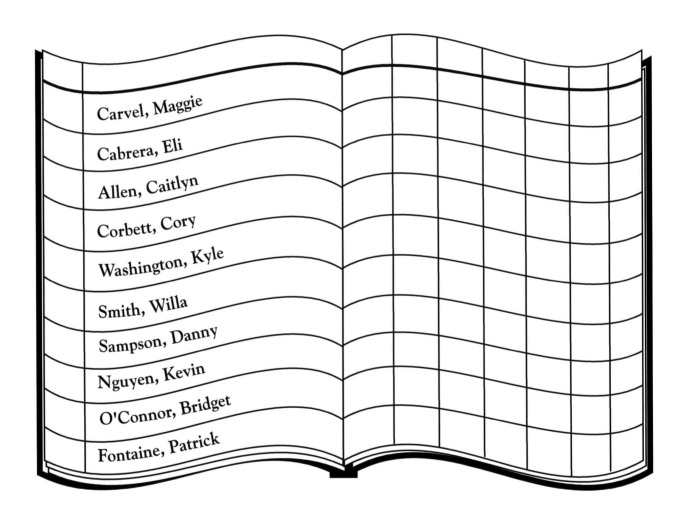

Carvel, Maggie

Cabrera, Eli

Allen, Caitlyn

Corbett, Cory

Washington, Kyle

Smith, Willa

Sampson, Danny

Nguyen, Kevin

O'Connor, Bridget

Fontaine, Patrick

Movie ABC

You are looking for a DVD in the video store. All of the DVDs are organized in **alphabetical order.** Read the title of the DVD that you are looking for, and then circle the location where you would find it.

1. Finding Nemo

   a. between Ernest Goes to Jail and Gone With the Wind

   b. between Beauty and the Beast and Ernest Goes to Camp

2. Olive's Big Adventure

   a. between Coming to America and Harriet the Spy

   b. between Harriet the Spy and When Harry Met Sally

3. The Rescuers Down Under

   a. between Under the Blue Sky and Zachary's Big Day

   b. between The Little Mermaid and Something to Talk About

4. Mulan

   a. between Harry Potter and the Sorcerer's Stone and Stand by Me

   b. between European Vacation and Gone With the Wind

5. Star Wars

   a. between Free Willy and Piglet's Big Movie

   b. between Piglet's Big Movie and Where the Red Fern Grows

157

Look It Up

Read the names in the telephone book pages below. Put the names in **alphabetical order** by numbering the names from 1 to 7. Write the correct number on the line. One has been done for you.

Mackey — Mason	86
_____ Madsen, Kyla 555-2455	
_____ Marsden, Johnathan 555-9034	
_____ Mason, Derek 555-0063	
_____ Mancini, Tracy 555-3482	
__1__ Mackey, Nora 555-0859	
_____ Marks, Frank 555-4987	
_____ Mancini, Anthony 555-4285	

Matheson — Mroz	87
_____ Merrill, Patty 555-1928	
_____ Mroz, Dean 555-3890	
_____ Merz, Miriam 555-2833	
_____ Merrill, George 555-9352	
_____ Matheson, Jane 555-4633	
_____ Moritz, Pam 555-0388	
_____ Matheson, Abigail 555-7765	

RESIDENCE LISTINGS

Order in the Books!

When you go into a library, the books are always arranged in **alphabetical order.** In order to find what you are looking for, you must know the alphabet. It is important to remember that words like *a, an,* and *the* are ignored when placing items in alphabetical order. For example, if the name of a book is <u>A Wizard's Life</u>, the word that determines how to alphabetize the book is *Wizard*.

Look around your classroom. Find eight books. Write the titles in alphabetical order.

1. _____

2. _____

3. _____

4. _____

5. _____

6. _____

7. _____

8. _____

Using a Dictionary

We use **dictionaries** to look up words that we don't know. Dictionaries help us in two ways. First, dictionaries show us how to spell words correctly. Second, dictionaries define, or tell the meanings of, words.

There are a few things that we have to know in order to use a dictionary. First of all, we need to know the alphabet. This helps us to look up things in the dictionary. Below are ten words. Read the words, and number them, 1 to 10, in alphabetical order.

_____ horse	_____ octopus
_____ xylophone	_____ zebra
_____ aardvark	_____ train
_____ carriage	_____ doctor
_____ softball	_____ hippopotamus

Now, choose five of the words above, and look them up in a dictionary. Write the definitions on the lines below.

11. _____

_____

12. _____

_____

13. _____

_____

14. _____

_____

15. _____

_____

Name_____

Parts of Speech

Dictionaries also tell us what part of speech a word is. That means that the dictionary tells us if the word is a **noun, verb, adjective,** and so forth. Below are a list of words. Some of these words can be different parts of speech. Using a dictionary, look up the words, and give all of the different parts of speech that the word may be.

1. run_____

2. swim_____

3. runaway_____

4. scout_____

5. side_____

6. foam_____

7. damp_____

Now, look up the words below. Write what part of speech the word is. Then, see if the word has any other forms. Choose one form. Write the form and its part of speech. The first one has been done for you.

8. dangerous _adjective; dangerously: adverb_____

9. humane_____

10. nasty_____

11. pain_____

12. selfish_____

Know the Dictionary

A **dictionary** gives you lots of information about a word. It tells how to spell a word, and gives all definitions, pronunciations, and parts of speech of the word. Sometimes the dictionary gives words with similar meanings called **synonyms.**

Example: laugh \ ter \ ′laf-ter \ *n*. the action or sound of laughing

Laughter is broken into two parts, or syllables. The next section shows how to pronounce the word. The accent mark on the first syllable shows that *laf* is stressed more than *ter*. Next, *n*. shows that the word is a noun. The definition of the word comes last.

Look up the following words in a dictionary, and write the number of syllables each word has. Then, write what part of speech the word is.

1. horse _____

_____

2. engine _____

_____

3. entire_____

_____

The Right Words

Using your **dictionary,** look up one word that begins with each of the letters below. Write the word and its definition.

1. A

_____

_____

2. L

_____

_____

3. X

_____

_____

4. Z

_____

_____

5. R

_____

_____

6. D

_____

_____

Dictionary Word Hunt

Find the following things in a **dictionary.** On the lines, write one or more words that fit the description given.

1. a word with three syllables _____

2. a word that has at least three different meanings _____

3. a word that can be a noun or a verb _____

4. a word that can be an adjective or an adverb _____

5. two words that have similar meanings _____

   _____

6. a word that begins with *x* _____

7. a word that has two acceptable spellings _____

Daily Skill-Builders Reading 3–4
walch.com © 2004 Walch Publishing

A Table of Contents

A **table of contents** tells you how parts of a book are arranged. A table of contents tells you on what pages you can find certain information.

Read the table of contents below. Then answer the questions that follow.

1. On what page does Chapter 3 begin? _____

2. If you finished Chapter 4, what page would you be on? _____

3. On what page does Chapter 5 begin? _____

4. If you wanted to read only Chapter 2, what pages would you read?

   _____

5. What is the title of Chapter 3? _____

6. What chapter contains information on wasps? _____

Using Your Textbooks

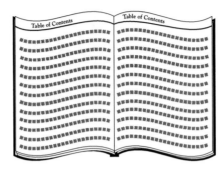

Choose one of your textbooks, and open it to the **table of contents.**

1. Is the table of contents divided into chapters? _____

2. How many chapters are in your book?_____

3. What chapter would you be in if you were on page 84? _____

4. How does the table of contents help you to find what you need? _____

_____

5. On what page does Chapter 1 start? _____

6. What is the last chapter of your book? _____

7. On what page does the last chapter start?_____

8. Is there a section in your book after the last chapter? If so, what is this section?

_____

Chapter by Chapter

Read the **table of contents** below, and answer the questions that follow.

Table of Contents

1. What is the title of Chapter 6? _____

2. On what page does the chapter called "Using Your Resources" begin? ____

3. Which chapter is titled "Prewriting and Planning"? _____

4. Which chapter begins on page 3? _____

5. What is the title of the chapter that begins on page 56? _____

6. Based on the information in the table of contents, what is the book

   about? _____

Life Story

Imagine that you are writing a story about your life. What would you write about? What exciting things have you done? Make a **table of contents** for your book. Be sure to title each chapter.

Table of Contents

_____

_____

_____

_____

_____

_____

1. On what page did you begin Chapter 3? _____

2. What is the title of your last chapter? _____

3. What is the title of your first chapter?_____

4. How many chapters are in your book?_____

5. What would you title your book?_____

Introducing the Index

An **index** is located in the back of a book. It contains information that is organized in alphabetical order. Each item in an index has a page number next to it to show where it can be found.

Study the index below. Then answer the questions that follow.

Index

A

aardvark 29

alligator 38

anaconda 87

anteater 101

antelope 13

B

baboon 23

badger 65

bear 99

bluebird 32

bobcat 14

---

1. To what page would you turn to find out about badgers? _____

2. What animal is discussed on page 99? _____

3. If you are on page 29, what animal are you reading about? _____

4. In the text, which animal is discussed just before the bobcat?

   _____

5. The animals are listed in alphabetical order in the index. Are they in alphabetical order within the text? _____

6. To what page would you turn to find out about anacondas? _____

7. Based on the index, what is the topic of this book? _____

Look It Up!

Indexes are organized in alphabetical order. Some books have different types of indexes. For example, if the book is a collection of short stories, it may have an author index and a title index. That way, if you know only the title and not the author, you can still look it up in the index.

Study the index below. Then answer the questions that follow.

Index

amethyst	74, 209
aquamarine	3
diamond	34, 35
emerald	5
pearl	86
peridot	28, 90
ruby	2, 90
sapphire	4, 73, 86

---

1. Are all of the words in the index arranged alphabetically? _____

2. Where would you look to find out about peridots? _____

3. On what page(s) could you read about amethysts? _____

4. What can be found on page 90? _____

5. Where can you find information about sapphires? _____

Daily Skill-Builders Reading 3–4
walch.com © 2004 Walch Publishing

Make Your Own Index

Below is a list of information in a book. Organize the words into an **index.** Be sure to put them in alphabetical order. Make up page numbers and write them as shown in the examples. The first few have been done for you.

~~basketball~~	skiing	lacrosse	~~badminton~~
swimming	tennis	rowing	running
~~baseball~~	~~boxing~~	wrestling	walking
hockey	soccer	golf	

B

badminton 34

baseball 10

basketball 22

boxing 59

1. On what page would you find information about rowing? _____

2. On what page would you find information about swimming? _____

3. On what page would you find information about boxing? _____

4. What is this book about? _____

Where Does It Go?

Indexes are organized in alphabetical order. Some books have different types of indexes. For example, if the book is a collection of literature, it may have an author index and a title index. That way, if you know only the title and not the author, you can still look it up in the index.

Below is a list of information that needs to be organized into an index. There are two indexes for this book. One is for titles and the other is for authors. Write the information in the appropriate index. Don't forget to organize the information alphabetically and add the correct punctuation to book titles.

Crane, Stephen	98	Mailer, Liz	37
The Swing	101	The Farmhouse	48
Silverstein, Shel	35	Reali, Samuel	57
Golding, William	22	By the Sea	119
Mama's House	12	The House on Smith Street . .	39
Angelou, Maya	53	Matt's Big Adventure	28
Waiting for Love	94	Mason, Michael	63

Titles

_____

_____

_____

_____

_____

_____

Authors

_____

_____

_____

_____

_____

_____

Using Encyclopedias

An **encyclopedia** is a book or set of books that contains information on many different subjects. The entries in an encyclopedia are arranged alphabetically by subject.

Your teacher has asked you to research an animal and write a short paragraph about it. You may choose any animal. However, everyone needs to use the encyclopedias. Here are three encyclopedias that you can use.

Volume 1

A–Cre

Volume 8

Her–Mef

Volume 14

Sea–Umb

1. Which volume of the encyclopedia would you use to research seals?_____

2. If you use Volume 8, what are some animals you could research?

_____

3. Could you research sea lions using these three books? _____

4. Could you research zebras using these three books? _____

5. What are some animals you could find in Volume 1?_____

_____

Where Is It?

Below is a set of **encyclopedias.** Using the information on the encyclopedias, answer the questions that follow.

A– Cre Vol. 1	Cri– Dor Vol. 2	Dra– Fre Vol. 3	Fri– Jar Vol. 4	Jas– Mar Vol. 5	Mas– Q Vol. 6	R– The Vol. 7	Thi– Wed Vol. 8	Wel– Z Vol. 9

1. How many volumes are in this set of encyclopedias? _____

2. In what volume could you read about the United States? _____

3. What part of the alphabet does Volume 3 cover? _____

4. Where would you look up icicles? _____

5. Where would you look up France?_____

6. Where would you look up Peru? _____

7. Where would you look up zebras? _____

8. How is an encyclopedia organized? _____

_____

Read It Here

An **encyclopedia** is a great resource. It has information about lots of different topics. Below is an example of what you may read in an encyclopedia. Read the paragraph. Then answer the questions that follow.

North America

North America is a continent. It is made up of the United States, Canada, Mexico, and Central America. There are seven countries in Central America. Some islands in the Caribbean are also considered part of North America. Canada is the largest country in North America. North America is varied. There are many different cultures, landforms, languages, and animals. North America is a unique place.

---

1. Are North America and Central America two different continents?

_____

2. How many countries are in there in Central America? _____

3. What country in North America is the largest? _____

4. Is Canada part of North America? _____

What Is an Almanac?

An **almanac** is a book containing a calendar of days, weeks, and months. It usually has facts and predictions about days. It usually has information about the weather and the sun and the moon.

Below is an example of a page from an almanac.

Special Days

Valentine's Day:	February 14
St. Patrick's Day:	March 17
May Day:	May 1
Cinco de Mayo:	May 5
Mother's Day:	Second Sunday in May
Father's Day:	Third Sunday in June
Halloween:	October 31
Kwanza:	December 26

---

1. What date is St. Patrick's Day? _____

2. In what month is Mother's Day? _____

3. When is Father's Day? _____

4. Does Valentine's Day fall on the same date every year? _____

5. Does Cinco de Mayo fall on the same day each year? _____

6. When is Kwanza? _____

Using an Almanac

An **almanac** is a book containing a calendar of days, weeks, and months. It usually has facts and predictions about days. It usually has information about the weather and the sun and the moon.

Almanacs may also have collections of random information. They may have world records, different conversion charts, and so on.

Read the information in the conversion chart below. Then answer the questions that follow.

Conversion Chart

Metric System		English System
1 centimeter or 10 millimeters	=	0.3937 inch
1 decimeter or 10 centimeters	=	3.937 inches
1 meter or 10 decimeters	=	39.37 inches or 3.28 feet
1 decameter or 10 meters	=	393.7 inches

1. One meter equals how many decimeters? _____

2. 393.7 inches equals how many meters? _____

3. How many centimeters are in one decimeter? _____

4. How many meters are in one decameter? _____

5. One decimeter equals how many inches? _____

177

What's the Weather?

An **almanac** is a book containing a calendar of days, weeks, and months. It usually has facts and predictions about days. It usually has information about the weather and the sun and the moon. Almanacs may have world records, different conversion charts, facts about countries and continents, lists of presidents, and many other kinds of quick facts.

Below is a calendar from an almanac. It has weather predictions for the month of December. Study the calendar, and answer the questions that follow.

December

Sunday	Monday	Tuesday	Wednesday	Thursday	Friday	Saturday
		1	2	3	4	5￼ hail storm
6	7	8	9￼ half moon	10	11	12
13	14￼ 6" of snow	15	16	17	18	19
20	21￼ 9" snow	22	23￼ winter solstice	24	25	26￼ 18" of snow
27	28	29	30	31		

1. When is the first storm of December expected? _____

2. December 26 is Boxing Day. What is the weather going to be like on

   Boxing Day? _____

3. On what date does the winter solstice fall? _____

4. When is the first snowstorm in December expected? _____

The Best Source

Sometimes you need (or want!) to learn about something that you don't know about. There are lots of different resources that you can use. Below is a list of **reference books** that you may use.

Dictionary: a book that gives the spelling and definitions of words

Thesaurus: a book that gives synonyms and antonyms of words

Encyclopedia: a book that gives general information about a variety of subjects

Almanac: a book that tells about days, weeks, and months of the year, weather predictions, world statistics, sports records, and other quick-fact types of information

Read the questions below. Where would you locate the information you are asked to find?

1. What is the weather going to be like on August 27? _____

2. What is the spelling of *amphibian*? _____

3. What does *caucasian* mean? _____

4. When did Hawaii become a state? _____

5. What is the capital of Argentina? _____

6. What is another word for *nice*? _____

7. How do you pronounce *hyperbole*? _____

8. What is another word for *scary*? _____

To What Does It Refer?

There are many different types of **reference books.** Below are entries from different types of books. Read the entry, and then decide if it is from a **dictionary,** a **thesaurus,** an **encyclopedia,** or an **almanac.**

1. the • ater \'the-et-er\ *n.* a building where plays or movies are shown

    _____

2. There will be a full moon on Thursday, June 26.

    _____

3. **nice:** pleasant, pleasing, well-behaved, agreeable, friendly

    _____

4. **night:** \'nit\ *n.* the time between dusk and dawn when the sun is not shining

    _____

5. North America

    A continent made up of the United States, Canada, Mexico, Central America, and some Caribbean islands. Canada is the largest country in North America.

    _____

Answer Key

READING COMPREHENSION

Page 1: Drawing Directions
The student should have drawn a picture with grass, 2 trees, 5 birds, a person standing under a tree, and a sun, as indicated in the directions.

Page 2: Pop Quiz!
Students should answer ONLY questions 1, 3, 6, and 7.

Page 3: Derek Goes to Work
1. The following names should be circled: Joanie, Ms. Matheson, James, Nancy. 2. 9:00 A.M. should be underlined. 3. desk, chair, telephone, and computer

Page 4: Scavenger Hunt
Note: Crayons, markers, or colored pencils are needed for this activity. Answers will vary. Objects should be colored correctly.

Page 5: Why Should I Listen?
1. FOLLOWING DIRECTIONS IS VERY IMPORTANT. 2. DRAW A SAILBOAT IN THE BOX. Sudents should draw a sailboat in the box provided.

Page 6: State Search

J	M	E	L	F	K	M	I	C	H	I	G	A	N	L
F	L	O	R	I	D	A	Y	O	U	A	I	O	W	N
N	A	R	N	P	S	S	E	R	K	H	W	P	Q	M
E	Z	I	A	L	A	S	K	A	U	W	S	A	Z	I
W	B	D	N	T	I	A	L	R	E	T	C	F	I	S
M	A	I	N	E	G	C	O	L	O	R	A	D	O	I
E	H	L	E	X	D	H	K	T	F	L	H	A	S
X	O	L	V	A	M	U	Y	B	I	H	I	O	D	L
I	C	I	A	S	H	S	W	Y	O	O	F	K	W	P
C	X	N	D	F	C	E	N	E	W	Y	O	R	K	O
O	Z	O	A	T	B	T	P	C	B	D	R	J	E	F
Y	A	I	N	R	Y	T	S	M	A	I	N	O	D	N
E	N	S	A	A	L	S	T	K	J	H	I	B	S	T
R	H	O	D	E	I	S	L	A	N	D	A	N	Y	S

Page 7: Recipe for Disaster
1. Mario didn't let the cake cool. 2. He thought that he was finished after baking the cake. 3. We should read ALL of the directions.

Page 8: Favorite Foods Graph
Note: Crayons, markers, or colored pencils are needed for this activity.
1. Pizza should be colored red. 2. French fries should be colored blue. 3. Hot dogs should be colored green.

4. Hamburgers should be colored yellow. 5. Ice cream should be colored brown.

Page 9: Make Your Own Circle Graph
Note: Crayons, markers, or colored pencils are needed for this activity.

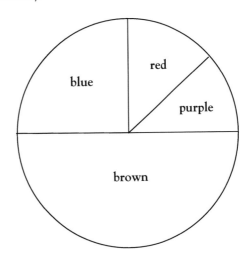

Page 10: Ordering Carly's Day
1. c 2. f 3. h 4. a 5. e 6. b 7. d 8. g

Page 11: Birthday Cake Order
1. a 2. f 3. c 4. e 5. g 6. h 7. d 8. b

Page 12: Skiing Sequence
1. He went to the rental department. 2. He met his father for lunch. 3. with his dad 4. He fell asleep in the car.

Page 13: Fish Magnets
1. c 2. e 3. b 4. f 5. a 6. d 7. g

Page 14: Florida Sequence
1. to Sea World 2. watched the trick water skiiers 3. went to Shamu's show 4. bought a stuffed Shamu doll for Kasey

Page 15: Order on the Farm
1. chicken 2. sheep 3. ducks 4. horses 5. pigs 6. cows

Page 16: Your Sequence
Answers will vary.

Page 17: What a Long Day!
1. b 2. a 3. c 4. e 5. g 6. f 7. d 8. h

Page 18: Fish Sequence
Note: Crayons, markers, or colored pencils are needed for this activity.
The fish next to the following statements should be colored: 1. Preheat the oven to 350°. 2. Take off your socks. 3. Eat dinner. 4. Put on your winter coat. 5. Go to

kindergarten. 6. Go for a swim in the lake. 7. Get home from school.

Page 19: A Picture Is Worth 1,000 Words
Possible answers:
1. The cat is chasing the mouse. 2. Billy is rounding first base. 3. Jill is waking up. 4. Sue won the race.

Page 20: Finding the Main Idea
1. Abraham Lincoln 2. He was a president who wanted to abolish slavery; he was assassinated. 3. Suggested sentence: *Abraham Lincoln was an important president.*

Page 21: Holiday Spirit
1. Mrs. Keene's fifth-grade class 2. collecting toys for needy kids 3. because some families didn't have enough money for gifts 4. "Helping Needy Families" 5. Toys were collected through December 15.

Page 22: A Maine Event
1. Mr. Bishop's fourth-grade class 2. The class went on a whale-watching trip. 3. They were studying marine wildlife. 4. "Watching Maine Whales"

Page 23: Whose Idea Was That?
Answers may vary.
1. birthday 2. animals or zoo 3. rocks and minerals 4. U.S. presidents 5. the beach

Page 24: Don't Bug Me!
1. c 2. Answers will vary.

Page 25: Kalisha's Summer
Possible answers:
II. I visited three places during my vacation.
III. I learned to do many things.
IV. I ate my favorite foods this summer.

Page 26: Your Autobiography
Answers will vary.

Page 27: All About Elephants
1. Elephants are fascinating creatures. 2. Answers will vary. 3. in Africa and Asia 4. to get their ivory to sell

Page 28: Feathered Friends
1. to Florida, to a bird sanctuary 2. because Toni is referred to as a "she" 3. 6 4. flamingo

Page 29: Camping Details
1. last summer 2. in the White Mountains 3. They drove there. 4. after they set up their tent 5. 5

Page 30: Detailed Description
Possible answers:
1. This frog has dark spots. The contrasting colors are a warning to other animals to stay away. 2. The magician has left her hat and magic wand behind. Her rabbit is not sure whether he should stay in or hop out of the stuffy hat.

3. There are so many pancakes on the plate that the sticky maple syrup has poured over the edge and pooled on the table.

Page 31: Picnic in the Park
Sample paragraph:
Last Sunday started out bright and sunny. My mother, father, brother, and I decided to go to the park. We saw a mother duck with six babies. The fluffy, yellow ducklings were so cute! Then we spread out a soft blanket and had a picnic of peanut butter and jelly sandwiches, carrots, and lemonade. We had to cut our picnic short when dark clouds, thunder, and lightning drowned out the sun. We packed up the rest of our picnic and hurried to the car just as it started to rain.
Possible titles: "An Almost Perfect Picnic" or "Just in the Nick of Time."

Page 32: Dad's Chocolate Chip Cookies
1. Monday 2. freshly baked, warm, gooey 3. good, because the narrator says that he or she loves the scent 4. Answers will vary.

Page 33: Details of Your Hand
Descriptions will vary.

Page 34: Describe Your Friend
Descriptions will vary.

Page 35: Details, Details!
The following words should be circled:
1. long, fluffy 2. vivid, blue 3. soft, velvety 4. coarse, hay 5. deep, foghorn 6. slippery, pointed, rainbow 7. heavy, moist 8. Answers will vary.

Page 36: Tell Me More!
Possible answers:
1. I live in the wonderful and beautiful United States. 2. John has big, floppy feet. 3. Kareem has sparkling, deep brown eyes. 4. We went for an exciting boat ride on the deep, wide lake. 5. The mountains were big and dangerous, and they were covered with deep drifts of white snow. 6. The large dog was very black with a few round, white spots on it. 7. The ranch house was a light yellow with dark blue shutters. 8. It was a blustery, windy day with leaves blowing all over the place.

Page 37: What Am I?
1. a sofa 2. a bird 3. a fish 4. a cloud 5. a book 6. a flower 7. drums

Page 38: What to Conclude?
1. the sun 2. an umbrella 3. a tree

Page 39: Aisha's Conclusion
1. the zoo 2. fish, birds, cages with tigers and lions, penguins, walruses, whales, and elephants 3. Answers will

vary, but may include titles such as "A Special Surprise" or "A Day of Fun."

Page 40: What Could I Be?
1. a rabbit 2. a bird 3. a fish 4. a tree 5. a letter
6. a computer

Page 41: How Do You Know?
1. She is very happy and surprised; no 2. probably 3. There is going to be a thunderstorm; probably not; because the wind is blowing and there is thunder

Page 42: Calendar Conclusions
1. dance class 2. Sunday 3. yes 4. April 24 5. ski lesson
6. April 30 7. flute lesson

Page 43: Take a Guess
1. a dolphin 2. a zebra 3. a flamingo 4. a monkey
5. a kangaroo 6. a giraffe 7. a polar bear

Page 44: Why Did That Happen?
1. He is all stuffed up, his nose is running, he is sneezing, and he is having trouble breathing. 2. He is at a cabin that his family rented. 3. There had been a cat at the cabin.
4. Marcus is allergic to cats, and he is having an allergic reaction.

Page 45: What Will Happen?
1. Shana will fall off her bike. 2. Sadie doesn't think that Shana is ready to ride a bike without training wheels.
3. Sadie told Shana that she didn't think that she was ready. Sadie removes the training wheels "against her better judgment."

Page 46: What's Next?
1. Timothy is going to fall in. 2. Timothy's father tells him not to lean over so far, but he does it anyway. 3. The seeds will grow into plants. 4. They water and care for the seeds every day.

Page 47: Predicting Plots
Possible answers:
1. Mrs. Jones takes her class to the zoo. The class rides the zoo train and eats lunch there. 2. On our Arizona vacation, we had a day to remember. We rode mules to the bottom of the Grand Canyon. 3. Jim and Jake had a wild and wacky adventure. They took a raft trip down a river and fell overboard. 4. Everywhere there are talking cats. They are planning to attack a dog pound and set the dogs free.

Page 48: Picture Predictions
Possible answer:
There will be a storm.

Page 49: Super Predictions
Possible answers:
1. Gavin goes to school, as usual. 2. Gavin makes friends

with a boy new to the school. 3. Corey, Gavin's new friend, gets lost on his way home from school. 4. Gavin has a hunch that Corey may have wound up in Dramble Forest. 5. Gavin finds Corey by a stream. 6. Gavin leads Corey home.

Page 50: How Do You Know?
1. Mary Ann is going to fall because her shoes are too slippery. 2. The chair is going to fall into the water because the wind is blowing and the chair is on the edge.
3. Abby is going to get a sunburn because she forgot to put on her sunscreen.

Page 51: What's the Outcome?
1. c 2. e 3. g 4. f 5. a 6. h 7. d 8. b

Page 52: Predicting the Future
Possible answers:
1. He became an expert in math. He gets a good grade on his test. He gets to represent his class in a math contest.
2. The river is rising. The yard is muddy. Peter had trouble sleeping because of the noise. 3. Students are looking forward to vacation. Gena's family is planning a family trip. Maria is looking forward to playing baseball. 4. Ginny is an excellent player. Ginny becomes team captain. Ginny's team beats Mabel's team.

Page 53: Cause and Effect
1. b 2. d 3. g 4. f 5. a 6. c 7. e

Page 54: What's the Cause?
Possible answers:
1. The keys were left in an amusement ride. 2. Shirley got a new kitten. 3. Betty fell off the step. 4. The baby is hungry. 5. The guitarist turned up the amplifier. 6. The carton of juice fell off the counter. 7. The ball hit a window. 8. A wind storm blew through town.

Page 55: What's the Effect?
Possible answers:
1. The sandcastle washed away. 2. Danny failed the test.
3. Kristin's team photo appeared in the paper. 4. Her glasses were shattered. 5. I fell asleep. 6. The sky became dark. 7. We had a day off from school—a snow day! 8. The dog barked.

Page 56: Special Effects
2. the wind blew; the leaves right off the tree 3. the loud music; kept me awake 4. her tail got shut in the door; our cat meowed 5. I fell off my bike; skinned my knee
6. I forgot my jacket at school; I shivered 7. The pavement was hot; I burned my feet 8. The wave crashed over the boat; soaked us 9. I had been walking so long; my feet hurt
10. we lost our electricity; the lights went out

Page 57: Why Did That Happen?
1. She bent her finger. 2. His friends jumped out and surprised him. 3. He slipped on a banana peel. 4. She went to sleep on her stomach in the sun.

Page 58: It Makes No Sense!
2. correct 3. correct 4. incorrect 5. correct 6. incorrect 7. correct 8. correct

Page 59: Cause or Effect?
Possible answers:
1. storm damage 2. no school 3. exhausted person 4. broken leg 5. made baseball team 6. boat ride in rough water 7. hit by a ball 8. fell on a sharp rock 9. forgot to water flowers 10. hungry

Page 60: The Effect of Flowers
Possible answers:
1. Roads are plowed. School is closed. Events are canceled. Walks need to be shoveled. 2. Grades are higher. Know more about the subject. Learn good studying skills to use later. 3. Have someone to play with. Have someone to study with. Have a new place to go. 4. Honey bees make honey. People get stung. Plants get pollinated.

Page 61: Fact Versus Opinion
1. fact 2. opinion 3. fact 4. opinion 5. fact 6. fact 7. opinion 8. opinion

Page 62: What's Your Opinion?
Possible answers:
1. School days are too long. 2. Reading is a great subject. 3. Tigers are beautiful. 4. Birds are always hungry. 5. My friends are clever. 6. Math is difficult. 7. Soccer is the best sport for kids to play.

Page 63: Finding Facts
The following numbers should be circled: 2, 5, 6, 7. The following statements should be underlined: 1, 3, 4, and 8.

Page 64: At the Dude Ranch!
1. fact 2. fact 3. fact 4. opinion 5. opinion 6. fact 7. opinion 8. fact 9. opinion

Page 65: Give Me the Facts!
1. Ethan 2. Brendan 3. The only information that Ethan gave—about the Colorado River—can be proved to be true. The statements Brendan made were about his personal experience and, although he felt them to be true for him, they might not be true for everyone.

Page 66: Fact or Fiction?
1. opinion; fact 2. fact; opinion 3. fact; opinion 4. fact; opinion 5. fact; opinion 6. fact; opinion 7. fact; opinion

Page 67: School Fact Check
Possible answers:
1. My school is almost one mile from my house. 2. It is a large brick building. 3. It has twenty classrooms. 4. My teacher is Ms. Harris. 5. It has a cafeteria. 6. My school is the best in town. 7. My school has the best teachers. 8. There are too many students in my school. 9. Classrooms should all be on one floor. 10. School should start later and end earlier. 11. Answers will vary.

Page 68: Is That a Fact?
Possible answers:
1. Bill Clinton was president of the United States. 2. Golden retrievers are a kind of dog. 3. Baseball is a popular sport. 4. We have picnics in the park. 5. I live in New England. 6. My family spends Sundays on our boat. 7. We skate in the winter. 8. Winter is one season.

Page 69: Fruit or Vegetable?
Possible answers:
1. Fruit, a major food group, should be eaten daily. There are many different kinds of fruit, including tomatoes. 2. Sentences will vary.

Page 70: Summarizing Summer
Answers will vary.

Page 71: Too Many Words
Possible answers:
1. Beth reads books every chance she gets. 2. Leo loves to snowboard. 3. There are many kinds of dogs.

Page 72: Tennis Summary
1. singles and doubles 2. a racket and a ball 3. Wimbledon and the US Open 4. Pete Sampras, Venus Williams, and Andre Agassi 5. *Possible summary:* Tennis is a sport that is enjoyed by many people. Some players are amateurs, and some are professional athletes.

Page 73: Summarizing March
1. dinosaurs 2. 2 3. 2 4. The class is studying dinosaurs.

Page 74: A New Snow White
Possible answers:
1. Every dwarf got to speak three lines. They practiced for a whole week. 2. No, they add information, but are not vital to understanding the main idea—the work that went into getting ready for the play. 3. Mr. O'Brien's class rewrote "Snow White." They performed their play for the whole school.

Page 75: Where to Visit?
Answers will vary.

Page 76: No Homework!
1. She doesn't have her homework done. 2. She doesn't want to get in trouble. 3. Yes, it would have been difficult

for her to do her homework given the fact that her mother was in labor and Lauren was not at home.

Page 77: Let's Get Together
Possible answers:
1. red, blue, green, brown, yellow 2. baseball, soccer, tennis, football, golf 3. George W. Bush, Queen Elizabeth, Sammy Sosa, Madonna, Oprah Winfrey 4. dog, cat, pig, cow, horse

Page 78: Whom Do You Know?
Answers will vary.

Page 79: Things in Common
1. colors 2. drinks 3. movies 4. bugs 5. hair colors 6. cities 7. amusement parks 8. shoes 9. desserts 10. teams 11. countries 12. sports

Page 80: Up, Up, and Away!
1. sad, happy, excited, scared 2. Albany, Boston, Oklahoma City, Sacramento 3. eagle, blue jay, chickadee, hawk 4. rose, lily, daisy, orchid

Page 81: We Belong Together
1. pants 2. sports 3. trees 4. states 5. dogs 6. vehicles

Page 82: Making Connections
1. Mel Gibson, Brad Pitt, Britney Spears, Backstreet Boys 2. Pacific Ocean, Atlantic Ocean, Lake Michigan, Mississippi River 3. corduroys, socks, jeans, T-shirt 4. coffee, lemonade, soda, milk 5. Mark, Jonathan, Michael, Paul 6. sand, starfish, sunscreen, seashells

Page 83: Genres
1. a 2. a 3. b 4. a 5 and 6. Answers will vary.

Page 84: Birds of a Feather
1. dinosaurs 2. insects 3. birds 4. shellfish

Page 85: Same and Different
Possible answers:
Compare: animals, four legs, tails, body markings
Contrast: height, mane, type of tail, length of neck

Page 86: Livie and Jade
1. They live in the same neighborhood. They ride their bikes together. They go to the same elementary school. They play together at recess. 2. They are in different classes. Livie loves to read, and Jade loves math. Livie's birthday is in March; Jade's is in April.

Page 87: Sibling Differences
Sample paragraph:
Julia doesn't like math. She is short. She has dark hair and dark eyes. She is loud and outgoing. She is not a very good student, but she loves school.

Page 88: Compare Yourself
Answers will vary.

Page 89: Dogs Versus Cats
The cat is wild, but the dog is pretty mellow. The cat climbs all over everything, but the dog lies around all day. Both animals race around after dinner. The cat has short hair, but the dog has long hair. Both of them shed all over the house.

Page 90: Where's the Contrast?
1. b 2. e 3. h 4. i 5. a 6. g 7. d 8. j 9. f 10. c

Page 91: Joey's Journal
Possible answer:
On Thursday, Joey went on a field trip, and on Friday he was at school. On Friday, Joey talked about his trip to the museum. Joey had a better time Thursday than Friday.

Page 92: What's the Connection?
1. different 2. similar 3. different 4. different 5. similar 6. different

Page 93: At the Zoo!
1. polar bears 2. picnic area 3. refreshments 4. tigers 5. at the center of the zoo

Page 94: Mapping the Classroom
1. right 2. Room 109 3. Rooms 104, 105 4. Rooms 103, 107, 108 5. the gym

Page 95: My Neighborhood Map
1. Congress 2. Johnson 3. Congress, Maple, Johnson, Oak 4. Forest 5. Forest, Dixon

Page 96: Charting Grades
1. Roberto 2. Roberto, Kyle, Dustin 3. October 27 4. Kate 5. Roberto, T.J., Kristie, Sophie

Page 97: Movie Chart
1. 1:20 2. 1:00 3. 8:15 4. The Rocking Skaters 5. The Mighty Frogs, The Rocking Skaters 6. 3:40 7. The Weasel and the Groundhog

Page 98: Charting Our Pizza
1. 10 2. Zachary 3. Valerie and Connor 4. 8 5. Patty 6. Li and Mattie 7. $5 8. Valerie and Connor

Page 99: Flight Chart
1. Flight 3509 2. From Boston 3. to Ft. Lauderdale 4. 1025, 2400, 1017 5. 3509 6. 2400

Page 100: Venn Diagram
1. 10 2. 8 3. 4

Page 101: Eye on the Diagram
1. optic nerve 2. lens 3. cornea 4. the eye

Page 102: Heart to Heart
Note: Crayons, markers, or colored pencils are needed for this activity. Parts of the heart should be colored appropriately.

Page 103: My House
1. 2 2. living room, kitchen, and dining room 3. 3 4. 4
5. the second floor

Page 104: What's the Weather?
1. cloudy/overcast 2. hail 3. 22% of the time 4. sunshine
5. sleet

Page 105: Graphing Progress
1. 60 2. September 29 3. September 1 4. 80

Page 106: Bookworms
1. 25 2. February 3. December and January 4. 20

Page 107: Ms. Wilson's Day
1. science 2. 25% 3. 25% 4. art, recess, and lunch 5. no
6. 18%

ELEMENTS

Page 108: What a Character!
1. Trey 2. yes 3. yes 4. Mrs. Cohen 5. Answers will vary.

Page 109: Zoo Characters
1. Loni 2. yes 3. Loni's mother and Stuart

Page 110: Writing in Character
Answers will vary.

Page 111: Character Search
1. Tammy 2. The story starts with her and what she is
doing. 3. Harry and Georgie

Page 112: Kelly in Kindergarten
1. Kelly 2–5. Answers will vary.

Page 113: Know Your Characters
1. Johnny is not a pleasant character. 2. Answers will vary.
3. The author doesn't really like Johnny. 4. spoiled, on
purpose, talked back 5. Caleb is a brave character.
6. Answers will vary. 7. The author probably admires
Caleb. 8. scared, courageous, brave.

Page 114: The Right Setting
1. d 2. a 3. e 4. c 5. b

Page 115: What's the Setting?
1. an amusement park 2. Milt 3. his mother 4. Germany
5. country town, farmers 6. Gretchen

Page 116: Describe the Setting
Answers will vary.

Page 117: Where Was That?
Possible answers:
1. hospital 2. school 3. grocery store 4. restaurant 5. street
6. kitchen

Page 118: Brainstorming Plots
Answers will vary.

Page 119: Haunted Plot
1. The boys go to the haunted house on Halloween.
2. Nate 3. Answers will vary.

Page 120: Your Own Book
Answers will vary.

Page 121: Plotting Books
1. c 2. d 3. a 4. e 5. b 6–7. Answers will vary.

Page 122: Plot Sequence
Answers will vary.

Page 123: Who's Talking?
1. third 2. first 3 third 4. third 5. first 6. third 7. first
8. first

Page 124: Australian Point of View
Answers will vary. Letter should be written in first person.

Page 125: View from the Sky
Numbers 1, 4, 7, and 9 should be circled. Sentences in
clouds 2, 3, 5, 6, and 8 should be underlined.

Page 126: What's the Point of View?
Possible answers:
1. I like to fish. 2. My dad and I fish together. 3. I catch
more fish. 4. Dick is always working. 5. He writes novels.
6. He works at a computer.

Page 127: View from the Big Top
1. 3 2. 1 3. 3 4. 1 5. 3

Page 128: Plymouth Rock
1. third person 2. 3 3. Jordan's mom 4. because it says
Jordan and **her** brother 5. Jordan's father

Page 129: Who Said That?
2. my mother and I 3. Jacinta and Jeff 4. the students
5. I 6. Luci 7. my mom and dad 8. sneakers

Page 130: Theme Stealing
1. the importance of honesty 2. The story teaches that it is
wrong to steal. 3. Answers will vary.

Page 131: Theme Versus Tone
Possible answers:
2. Many things happen that make people sad. 3. Everyone
gets angry at times, but they should learn to control their
responses. 4. Christmas is a holiday full of exciting events.
5. Ghost stories can scare a person.

Page 132: Your Theme Is . . .
Stories will vary.

Page 133: Writing to the Theme
Possible answers:
1. Money is nice, but friendship is priceless. 2. How lonely
we would be without family! 3. Honesty is a goal everyone

should hope to reach. 4. Loyalty often goes along with friendship.

Page 134: Why Read the Book?
1. family 2. honesty 3. patriotism 4. friendship

Page 135: Showing Tone
Possible answers:
2. I can't wait for Friday to come. Our class is going to the planetarium. 3. The story is so sad. I cried at the end. 4. I am anxious about being in the wedding. I hope I don't make a mistake. 5. The movie was very scary. It gave me nightmares.

Page 136: Watch Your Tone!
1. excitement 2. fear 3. excitement/anticipation 4. anger
5. nervous/anxious

Page 137: The Right Tone
1. f 2. e 3. a 4. d (or c) 5. b 6. c (or d)

Page 138: Tone It Down!
Possible answers:
1. happy: I am happy that we are going on vacation.
2. sad: I am sad my cat is lost. 3. worried: I'm afraid I won't do well in swim class. 4. angry: What a dumb thing I did today!

Page 139: Why Do We Read?
The following items should be circled: textbook, map, cookbook, atlas, owner's manual, worksheet, sheet music, board game rules. Students' own lists will vary.

Page 140: Why Read That?
1. enjoyment, information 2. enjoyment 3. information, instruction 4. information 5. instruction 6. enjoyment, information 7. information, instruction 8. information

Page 141: What Genre?
1. adventure 2. fantasy 3. biography 4. autobiography
5. mystery 6. adventure 7. fantasy 8. mystery

Page 142: Hunt for Genres
Answers will vary.

Page 143: Find a Better Word
Possible answers:
1. well-behaved 2. stifling 3. beautiful 4. gorgeous
5. exhausted 6. neat 7. sluggishly 8. quietly

Page 144: Word Scoops
Possible answers:
1. joyful, pleased 2. solemn, tearful 3. tiny, miniature
4. frightened, terrified 5. wonderful, lovely 6. beautiful, gorgeous

Page 145: More Words
Possible answers:
1. stormy, snowy, wintry, freezing, bone-chilling

2. friendly, affectionate, trusting, lovable, cuddly
3. fabulous, wonderful, engaging, exciting, great

Page 146: Does It Fit?
1. b 2. a 3. c 4. a 5. c

Page 147: Word Sense
1. sight 2. touch 3. smell 4. sound 5. taste
6. Sentences will vary.

Page 148: That Figures!
1. metaphor 2. simile 3. simile 4. metaphor 5. simile
6. simile 7. metaphor 8. simile

Page 149: Figures of Speech
1. s 2. c 3. none 4. n 5. p 6. Sentences will vary.

Page 150: Onomato . . . What?
The following words should be circled: clang, tick, zoom, bang, click, pop, boom, slap. Examples will vary.

Page 151: Figure It Out
1. simile 2. alliteration 3. onomatopoeia 4. metaphor
5. alliteration 6. onomatopoeia 7. simile

Page 152: Idioms
1. can't speak because of shyness 2. bad mood 3. go to bed
4. good luck 5. in a frenzied manner 6. think hard
7. raining really hard 8. get married

Page 153: Go Figure!
1. alliteration 2. simile 3. metaphor 4. onomatopoeia
5–8. Examples of figurative language will vary.

SKILLS

Page 154: Baby ABCs
1. Alex 2. Anthony 3. Connor 4. Darnell 5. Ethan
6. Garrett 7. Johnathan 8. Jordan 9. Malcolm 10. Mark
11. Matthew 12. Omar 13. Pedro 14. Ramon 15. Tyson

Page 155: Alphabetizing States
1. Alabama, Alaska, Arizona, Arkansas 2. California, Colorado, Connecticut 3. Idaho, Illinois, Indiana, Iowa
4. Maine, Maryland, Massachusetts, Michigan, Minnesota, Mississippi, Missouri, Montana

Page 156: Third-Grade Names
3, 2, 1, 4, 10, 9, 8, 6, 7, 5

Page 157: Movie ABC
1. a 2. b 3. b 4. a 5. b

Page 158: Look It Up
1, 2, 4, (3), 6, 9, 8, 5, 7, 11, 12, 13, 10, 14

Page 159: Order in the Books!
Answers will vary.

Page 160: Using a Dictionary
5 horse, 6 octopus, 9 xylophone, 10 zebra, 1 aardvark, 8 train, 2 carriage, 3 doctor, 7 softball, 4 hippopotamus; 11.–15. Words and definitions will vary.

Page 161: Parts of Speech
1. verb, noun 2. verb, noun 3. noun, adjective 4. verb, noun 5. noun, adjective, verb 6. noun, verb 7. noun, verb, adjective 9. humane: adjective; humanely: adverb; 10. nasty: adjective; nastily: adverb; nastiness, nasty: noun 11. pain: noun, verb; painless: adjective; painlessly: adverb; painlessness: noun 12. selfish: adjective; selfishly: adverb; selfishness: noun

Page 162: Know the Dictionary
1. one syllable; noun 2. two syllables; noun 3. two syllables; adjective

Page 163: The Right Words
Answers will vary.

Page 164: Dictionary Word Hunt
Possible answers:
1. runaway 2. rush 3. pain 4. very 5. nice, pleasing 6. xylophone 7. theater, theatre; tranquillity, tranquility

Page 165: A Table of Contents
1. page 37 2. page 71 3. page 72 4. pages 24–36 5. Roaches 6. 1

Page 166: Using Your Textbooks
1–8. Answers will vary. 9. Possible answers: glossary, index

Page 167: Chapter by Chapter
1. Proofreading and Editing 2. page 18 3. Chapter 2 4. Chapter 1 5. "Polishing Your Paper" 6. writing a research paper

Page 168: Life Story
Answers will vary.

Page 169: Introducing the Index
1. page 65 2. bear 3. aardvark 4. antelope 5. no 6. page 87 7. animals

Page 170: Look It Up!
1. yes 2. pages 28, 90 3. pages 74, 209 4. peridots and rubies 5. pages 4, 73, 86

Page 171: Make Your Own Index
badminton, baseball, basketball, boxing, golf, hockey, lacrosse, rowing, running, skiing, soccer, swimming, tennis, walking, wrestling 1–4. Answers will vary.

Page 172: Where Does It Go?
Titles: By the Sea, The Farmhouse, The House on Smith Street, Mama's House, Matt's Big Adventure, The Swing, Waiting for Love. Authors: Angelou, Maya; Crane, Stephen; Golding, William; Mailer, Liz; Mason, Michael; Reali, Samuel; Silverstein, Shel

Page 173: Using Encyclopedias
1. Volume 14 2. Answers will vary, but might include horse, javelina, kangaroo 3. yes 4. no 5. Answers will vary, but might include aardvark, bears, cows.

Page 174: Where Is It?
1. 9 2. Volume 8 3. Dra–Fre 4. Volume 4 5. Volume 3 6. Volume 6 7. Volume 9 8. It is in alphabetical order.

Page 175: Read It Here
1. no 2. 7 3. Canada 4. yes

Page 176: What Is an Almanac?
1. March 17 2. May 3. third Sunday in June 4. yes 5. no 6. December 26

Page 177: Using an Almanac
1. 10 2. 10 3. 10 4. 10 5. 3.937

Page 178: What's the Weather?
1. December 5 2. A snowstorm is predicted. 3. December 23 4. December 14

Page 179: The Best Source
1. almanac 2. dictionary 3. dictionary 4. encyclopedia or almanac 5. encyclopedia or almanac 6. thesaurus 7. dictionary 8. thesaurus

Page 180: To What Does It Refer?
1. dictionary 2. almanac 3. thesaurus 4. dictionary 5. encyclopedia or almanac